PHILOSOPHICAL ANALYSIS
IN EDUCATION

HARPER'S SERIES ON TEACHING

Under the Editorship of Ernest E. Bayles

PHILOSOPHICAL ANALYSIS IN EDUCATION

JOHN B. MAGEE

University of Puget Sound

HARPER & ROW, PUBLISHERS

New York, Evanston, San Francisco, London

PHILOSOPHICAL ANALYSIS IN EDUCATION
Copyright © 1971 by John B. Magee

Standard Book Number: 06-044164-X
LIBRARY OF CONGRESS CATALOG CARD NUMBER: 72-168350

TO KATHRYN

CONTENTS

EDITOR'S FOREWORD

The purpose, presumably, of stocking the mind is to secure retrieval of any one of the stored items when it is wanted. And, like a well-ordered library, retrieval is readily possible only when a well-ordered and easily understood filing system is in effect. Any worker who understands the system can then, at any time, go straight to a desired item, even though its location or even its existence was previously unknown to him. Logical deduction, not memory, serves as the locational principle.

Thought patterns represent the filing systems of the mind. To be able to "follow the run" of a thought pattern is to understand it. Broad principles or generalizations—high-level abstractions—

constitute thought patterns that have high retrieval value; they represent the kind of knowledge that makes transfer readily possible and enables a possessor to find it useful. The only genuinely practical subject-matter content a teacher can teach is basic, tested theory. And to think of philosophy as something other than broad, basic theory is probably to lose for philosophy any legitimate claim to a significant place in education.

Of extant philosophical systems, which furnishes the best organizational base for educational practice? This question is vital for an educational philosopher, and it seemingly should be of first importance for an educational practitioner. Chesterton, when asked whether it is important for a landlady to know a prospective tenant's philosophy of life, countered with the question, "Is anything else important?" This book is one in a series designed to furnish authentic presentations of major contemporary philosophies as they relate to, or impinge upon, educational practice. Each book takes a given philosophy and follows it into its impact or impacts upon such practice. Each author is presumed to be sympathetic to the view he presents and able to speak authoritatively for it. What each philosophy has to offer for education should therefore be discernible in the book devoted to it. Although the general editor and the publisher have not tried to tell any author how he should write his book, they are hopeful that this end will be served.

In addition, publication of the series in the form of separate paperbacks offers flexibility and economy in classroom use: An instructor is thus able thereby to select the specific views he wants studied, whether one or several, and require student purchases of those. Each book in the set is written with the expectation that the others will also be available—hence with no obligation to present any view but its own, even with the necessity perhaps, because of space limitation, to deal with that alone. We hope that the books in this series will prove highly useable and useful.

Ernest E. Bayles

PREFACE

Education is so great an enterprise and so big with promise or danger to man that any approach to it that can shed any light or brighten the prospects for its future in America and the world is worth exploring. Human reason takes many forms, and no school of philosophy can claim exclusive jurisdiction in so universal a concern, but since among educators philosophical analysis is so little understood or practiced, it has seemed to me eminently worthwhile to add a treatment of education from this point of view to the Harper & Row series on philosophy in education.

There are other ways of thinking philosophically about education, but I have tried to show the unique contribution that an analytic approach might make. I have discovered that there are some problems that yield best to this approach: for example, the clarifying of such major concepts as *teaching, learning,* and *educating.* Like pragmatism, analysis is closer to common sense than many other viewpoints and should appeal to the educator in somewhat the same way. It is a mode of philosophizing at which the educator can and should try his own hand once he becomes familiar with the "linguistic turn."

My thanks to the University of Puget Sound for allowing me a winter term to work on this book and to Miss Nancy Anderson for typing the manuscript.

J. B. M.

PART I
WHAT IS ANALYSIS

1

THE ANALYTIC REVOLUTION
IN PHILOSOPHY

An account of analytic philosophy is more difficult than summarizing schools of philosophy whose chief ideas have had time to come to definitive expression. One can write about Thomism, idealism, or pragmatism with confidence that authoritative interpretations are possible. Analytical philosophy, on the other hand, is still in the vital process of formulation. Its earlier stages can be recounted, but its current status is ambiguous and changes with each scholarly publication. Perhaps, within a couple of decades, it will achieve the kind of stability we associate with pragmatism.

There is a recompense. To write about a currently vital and developing philosophy provokes the excitement of joining in contemporary debates. It is not, however, my province to join the current dialogue over the validity of analytic philosophy. Our task is to see how this analytic way of doing philosophy can illuminate the field of education. Fortunately, this too is a living enterprise. Little more than a decade has passed since applications of analysis to educational theory have appeared in considerable number. Hardy's *Truth and Fallacy in Education* and O'Connor's *The Philosophy of Education*, were, I believe, the first full-scale works in the field.

Before discussing analysis in education, however, we should have a brief account of the beginnings of analysis in the early twenties, and the logic of the changes that have brought it to its present state.

ANALYSIS AS A PHILOSOPHICAL REVOLUTION

Analytical philosophers claim that in the second quarter of the twentieth century, English-speaking countries passed through a philosophical revolution of major proportions. Like the existentialists and phenomenologists on the European continent, philosophical analysts challenged, in the most basic way possible, the traditional role of philosophy. The success of this challenge in America can be measured, in part, by the fact that a majority of the teachers of philosophy in leading universities and colleges are now committed to an analytic way of doing philosophy.

Traditional philosophy was conceived as a rational investigation of the nature of reality, or as a way to solve human problems and to attain wisdom in human life. Its aspirations were global and synthetic. Philosophers in this tradition believed they were called to construct a world-view that would coherently encompass and illuminate every sphere of human thought and activity. Science, art, morality, politics, and religion were all grist for their mill.

Alfred North Whitehead, for example, one of the few system builders of the present century, in his *Process and Reality*, writes of the task of philosophy in these words: "Speculative Philosophy is the endeavour to frame a coherent, logical, necessary system of general ideas in terms of which every element of our experience can be interpreted."[1] He meant *every* element of experience, from common sense to natural science, from ethics and art to politics and religion.

In the modern West, the global program of philosophy was typically exemplified in the philosophies of Spinoza (1632–1677) and Hegel (1770–1831). Similarly, it was the aim of Aristotle in the ancient world and St. Thomas Acquinas (1227–1274) in medieval times. Even John Dewey (1859–1952), who proposed a universal methodology in place of a universal metaphysic, was inspired by the ideal of a total philosophy. He used the basic ideas of pragmatism to illuminate art, religion, ethics, and, most notably, education.

Over against these lofty conceptions of philosophy, analysts have come by various routes to the more modest view that the proper *role of philosophy is nothing more than the analysis of ordinary language* or the *analysis of concepts*.

G. E. Moore, professor of philosophy at Cambridge University from 1925 to 1939, proved to be prophetic. He claimed that in order to philosophize it was not necessary, as an expositor writes, "to have . . . nor to pretend to have . . . large scale metaphysical anxieties. It was necessary only to want to get things clear."[2]

To be sure, Moore was not a full-fledged linguistic analyst, but he laid the foundations for what has been called "the linguistic turn." According to this view, philosophical problems are odd puzzles created by philosophers. They may be solved or dissolved either by reforming language or by understanding the ordinary language that we use. Philosophers create puzzles when they wrongly assume that philosophy should explore the nature of *reality* and discover *truths* not known to scientists. In this, they unconsciously misuse language and create (instead of solutions) puzzles that are incomprehensible, insoluble, and artificial. The only remedy for this, say analysts, is to go back to the language from which these puzzles were constructed and show how they went astray.

[1] Alfred North Whitehead, *Process and Reality* (New York: Macmillan, 1963), p. 4.
[2] G. J. Warnock, *English Philosophy since 1900* (New York: Oxford University Press), p. 55. Richard Rorty, *The Linguistic Turn* (Chicago: University of Chicago Press, 1967). This is a fine collection of recent essays in analytic method.

THE METAPHYSICAL TRADITION

The great metaphysical schools each contended for a different answer to the question, "What is the nature of reality?" The scandal of their unresolvable disagreements is the open secret of philosophy. Idealists like Berkeley (1685–1753) postulated a universal *mind* as the basic reality. Such materialists as Hobbes (1588–1679) contended, on the contrary, that everything was really *matter*. Even *thought*, he said, was merely thin or tenuous material. Descartes (1596–1650) argued that reality was both *mind* and *matter*, each irreducible to the other. His puzzle about how two such different substances can interact in the human body led to a variety of strange and conflicting doctrines. Neo-Thomists, following St. Thomas Acquinas, who worked along the lines laid down by Aristotle, saw reality as a hierarchical structure with raw unformed matter at the base and pure spirit (God) at the top. Naturalists, on the contrary, contended that *nature* (defined in a variety of ways) is all there is.

This is, of course, a mere sampling, but it will suffice to illustrate the setting for a new departure. According to analysts, this chaos of contending schools, each unable to persuade its opponents of the truth of its view, left philosophy in an embarrassing disarray. Many thinkers came to view it as mere pseudolearning. What can be said, they ask, for an intellectual discipline that is congenitally unable to resolve its major problems and yet pretentiously lays claims to universal wisdom?

THE EPISTEMOLOGICAL TRADITION

The same puzzles greet us if we think of philosophy not as an attempt to find *reality*, but as an answer to the epistemological question, "How do we come to know?" Again, the schools fell into irreconcilable dispute. The rationalists said that the sovereign method for getting knowledge is through pure thought, reason alone. Using the model of mathematics (before its analysis by the great nineteenth-century mathematicians), they believed that the discovery of a few basic axioms would make possible a comprehensive system of knowledge that would be both clear and certain. In modern philosophy, the great names in this tradition are Descartes, Spinoza, and Leibniz (1646–1716). A glance at Spinoza's *Ethics*, with its propositions and proofs set out like Euclid's *Elements*, is an example of the deductive model that lured these thinkers. In the nineteenth century, Hegel invented a dialectical logic with which he hoped to break through into universal knowledge. The verdict of the critics is that these systems rest on unproven assumptions, and that the hope of learning about the world in this *a priori*[3] way is bound to fail.

The empiricists came to the rescue by appealing to *experience*. The way to reliable knowledge, they said, was to consult sense experience. Locke (1632–1704) held that there is nothing in the mind that is not first in the senses. Therefore, the way to clarify knowledge and to solve the ancient puzzles of philosophy is to trace ideas back to the sense experiences from which they sprang. Berkeley followed in Locke's steps and produced his famous refutation of materialism by showing that our notion of *matter* is nothing but a cluster of sense experiences (he called them "ideas"), such as *red, hard, hot, heavy,* and so on. And since, according to him, "ideas" could exist only in a mind, we must conclude that reality consists simply of minds and their contents.

Hume (1711–1776), Berkeley's successor, carried the empirical tradition to its logical conclusion. *Mind*, he showed, using the same arguments Berkeley had used against *matter*, was not a sense experience and was, therefore, merely a name for the bundle of sense experience we conventionally refer to as *mind*. He applied the same method to other notions like *objects* and *causality*. Concerning the latter, he observed that we never have sense impressions of causal connections. All we have is the experience of a fairly stable order of sensations, and that which we call "cause and effect" are merely the experienced regularities of life.

Dewey attempted another radical "reconstruction of philosophy" along different lines. The mistake of earlier philosophers, he said, was that they conceived of knowing as a passive reception of the world in which the mind performs somewhat like a camera. But, in fact, he argued, the human knower is really an organism adjusting

---

[3] *A priori* means "logically prior to and independent of sense experience." *A posteriori* means "derived from experience."

itself to its environment. The proper function of thought, according to Dewey, is reconstructing experience. Thoughts and beliefs should be looked upon as instruments in the struggle for existence, not as probes into the nature of reality. The fruit of this method, he and his followers believed, would give guidance for the solution of all types of human problems.

For the purposes of this short survey, it is not necessary to comment on the complex thought of the Kantian, Hegelian, or Marxian schools. They too had hoped to provide solutions to the problem of how we come to know what we know. In this way, they hoped to resolve the perennial problems of philosophy.

THE ANALYTIC CRITIQUE

Philosophical analysts claim no sovereign method for investigating reality. They hold the search for an epistemological solution to philosophical problems to be no more valid than the metaphysical tradition. The point is that the whole effort to find out what is "really real," or to think that philosophy can lead to a special wisdom of its own, is misguided. To ask "What is the nature of reality?" Or, "How do we know what we know?" is not to ask a genuine question. There is, therefore, no answer to them. The reason for this astonishing assertion follows. Whenever we ask meaningfully what is "real," we ask it in a specific context. Or, whenever, we ask how we know, we ask it of some specific thing: How do we know X? If we do not specify the context, the question is as yet incomplete and therefore unanswerable.

For example, we may ask, "What *really* happened when the two ships collided?" Or, "What *really* went on during the magic show?" Or, "What *really* caused the illness?" Or, "Is the oar *really* bent in the water?" All of these are questions that have possible answers. But when we ask, "What is really real?" we have left out all possible contexts, and therefore all meaning from the question. The reply to such a pseudoquestion is, "What are you talking about?"

Consider another example. Suppose someone were to ask, "How is the weather?" "Where?" you reply. "Oh, no place, just the weather in general, all weather." This query cannot be answered because though *it appears in the grammatical form of a meaningful question, it is not a question.*

The same problem arises in asking, "How do we know?" This question is incomplete. It should go like this: "How do we know X?" in which "X" refers to something that has meaning in a context. It is meaningful to ask, "How do we know that autistic children can learn?" Or, "How do we know that segregated schools lead to inferior education?" But, "How do we know?" is no question at all.

It is mistakes like this that have made philosophy a vast collection of puzzles that have no answers. Wittgenstein, one of the chief figures in the analytic revolution, said that the proper function of philosophy is to analyze such questions and dissolve them by showing their pseudocharacter. The inquiry concludes when the puzzle has disappeared. Thus, according to him, there are no philosophical doctrines of reality, no philosophical *truths*. When we are through philosophizing, everything is left "just as it is."

The parallel to psychoanalysis is illuminating. Therapy does not solve the problems of the neurotic or psychotic patient, it dissolves them so the patient can return to normal thinking and living. Before, the patient was confused, going round and round with his *problems*, whereas now he is free of them and recognizes them for what they were, pseudoproblems induced by his distorted way of perceiving the world. Philosophical analysis yields comparable therapy for many problems of classical philosophy.

If we look briefly at the way in which philosophical analysis emerged, it will further clarify what analysts believe to be the proper role of philosophy.

LOGICAL POSITIVISM AND THE BEGINNINGS OF ANALYSIS

After World War I, a group of European scholars whose chief interests lay in the natural and social sciences formed what became known as the Vienna Circle. They were disturbed by the way in which philosophy and science had become alienated. This has serious implications for an age in which science is the universally acknowledged means for the advancement of human knowledge.

The claims of philosophy on this score were becoming less and less convincing. The Circle began by conceding to science the claim to be the *only way* by which knowledge of the world can be attained. Any matter of fact must fall under one or another of the sciences. The testing of hypotheses through experiment and observation was the only way. Where does that leave philosophy? Their answer was that the proper role of philosophy is the analysis of the logical syntax of scientific language.

Scientists, for example, use such concepts as *law, explanation,* and *proof.* They also employ mathematics as their universal language. The task of philosophy, it appeared, was to clarify the meaning of these concepts, showing their logical structures and relationships. Any notion of "how the world is" was relegated to science, and the language used in science became the subject matter of philosophy.

This solved many problems at one stroke. It was no longer necessary to ask what special methods philosophy possessed for studying realities unknown to science. Philosophy received its subject matter secondhand from science, not as a superscience gathering all experience together into some kind of world synthesis, but as the logic of the language that scientists use in their inquiries. This task arose because science could not, by its own methods, examine the logic of its own methods.

The terms *logical positivism* or *logical empiricism* were derived from the fact that the language of science consists of two kinds of expressions, logical ones and empirical ones. An example of the former is mathematics. By itself, mathematics tells us nothing about the world. As Bertrand Russell once remarked, the mathematician does not know what he is talking about and, what's more, he does not care, because he is not talking about things in the real world. He deals with the relationships of ideal concepts, such as *lines, surfaces, spaces, numbers,* and the like.

Science is more than mere logic and mathematics; it makes contact with the world through sensory observations. Hence, the term *empiricism.* One of the problems of logical empiricism is then the relationship between observation language (the empirical element in science) and mathematical language (the logical element in science).

In their enthusiasm for their new discovery, the logical empiricists contended that all the traditional language of philosophy, where it talked about *values* or *reality, minds, matter,* or *God,* was meaningless, since such talk is neither empirical or logical. Expressions of this sort were called "emotive language."

"I will call metaphysical," wrote Rudolph Carnap, one of the leading members of the Vienna Circle, "all those propositions that claim to represent knowledge about something which is over or beyond all experience, for example, about the real Essence of things, about things in themselves, the absolute, and such like."[4] He explains what he means as follows: "What I have in mind are the doctrines of Realism, Idealism, Solipsism, Positivism and the like, taken in their traditional form as asserting or denying the reality of something."[5] He makes no attempt to argue against these views. As he says, ". . . we reject the whole question . . . our doctrine is a logical one and has nothing to do with metaphysical theses of the Reality or Unreality of anything whatever."[6] To be sure, these classical writers, as he says, "express something." But what they express is their own feeling, nothing that could be called "knowledge."

Another influential thinker of this period was Wittgenstein, whose *Tractatus Logico-Philosophicus,*[7] written independently of the Vienna Circle, and influenced in some measure by Russell, soon became virtually a bible of the new school of thought.

The *Tractatus* is cryptic and difficult to interpret. A relatively easier work, *Language Truth and Logic,*[8] written by Ayer in the midthirties, became a popular center around which debate centered. Much of the debate focussed on his formulation of the so-called verifiability criterion of meaning.

---

[4] Rudolph Carnap, "Philosophy and Logical Syntax," in Morton White (ed.), *The Age of Analysis* (New York: New American Library, 1955), p. 212.

[5] *Ibid.,* p. 214.

[6] *Ibid.,* p. 215–216.

[7] Ludwig Wittgenstein, *Tractatus-Philosophicus* (New York: Harcourt, Brace, 1922).

[8] A. J. Ayer, *Language Truth and Logic* (London, 1st Ed., 1935, 2nd Ed., 1946).

THE VERIFIABILITY CRITERION
OF MEANING

In its initial formulation, this notion appears simple enough. The meaning of a sentence, Ayer wrote, depends upon designating the way in which it can be verified. If I say, "This is a piece of iron," the meaning of the sentence depends upon the fact that there are palpable operations by which anyone competent in physics and chemistry can verify that it is indeed iron. But, if I say, "Capital punishment is immoral," I am not, according to Ayer, saying anything about the world. "Capital punishment" is, of course, meaningful in the verifiability sense. We can all specify instances that are cases of capital punishment. But when I have said it is *immoral*, to what empirically verifiable characteristics am I pointing? The grammatical form of the sentence seems to suggest that I have described it in some verifiable way, like saying it takes so long to perform, or it is executed by legally authorized officials. How can I point to its alleged "immoral" properties? Reasonable men, says Ayer, do not agree on propositions such as this because there is no way to verify the meaning of *immoral*.

For this reason, Ayer called all such statements "emotive." They reveal the feelings of the speaker, he said, but nothing about the thing itself. The statement "Capital punishment is immoral" can best be translated into some such form as "I, the speaker, don't *like* capital punishment." It tells us something about the psychology of the speaker, but not about the subject he appears to be talking about.

Using this criterion of meaning, Ayer was able, like Carnap, to relegate the whole tradition of metaphysics, ethics, and religion to the realm of emotive utterances. When a philosopher says that "reality is mental" or "reality is matter," he is saying something that cannot be verified and is therefore factually meaningless. What experiment or observation can one perform that would verify such statements? The very fact that philosophers have disputed these positions for so long is proof that they have no decisive empirical verification for their views. These statements, then, appearing to be claims about the world, are merely expressions of feeling about it.

The upshot of this line of argument led to the view that there are three kinds of language. There is *empirical* language that is about the world, and verifiable in the sense that Ayer contends. There is *analytical* (purely conceptual) language that is not about the world, but follows clear prescriptions for logical entailment. And there is *emotive* language.

Many questions soon gathered about the verifiability principle. For instance, it was asked, "Into which of the three kinds of language does the statement of the verifiability principle fall?" This is difficult to answer. If it is an *empirical* statement about how language is actually used, then it violates the principle that philosophy is not an empirical discipline like the sciences. If it is a purely analytical statement, then it is not about the world at all, only about concepts. In that case, it could not tell us about the meaning of meaning. And, of course, if it is an *emotive* statement, it tells us only about Ayer's feelings.

John Wisdom, one of the leading figures in analysis, wrote concerning this principle as follows: "Well, shall we accept the verification principle? What is it to accept it? When people bring out with a dashing air the words 'The meaning of a statement is really simply the method of its verification' . . . in what sort of way are they using words? What is the general nature of their theory? The answer is 'It is a metaphysical theory.' "[9] This is the ultimate in criticism, considering the logical empiricist's own condemnation of metaphysics as meaningless.

We need not go further into the details of this particular debate for the shift from logical empiricism to linguistic analysis came largely from another source.

THE SHIFT TO REDUCTIVE
(IDEAL LANGUAGE) ANALYSIS

By the midthirties, philosophers had reached a stage in the criticism of logical empiricism that proved to be an important transitional stage to ordinary language analysis. An understanding of this period

[9] J. O. Urmson, *Philosophical Analysis* (New York: Oxford University Press, 1956), pp. 169–170.

will clarify the meaning of contemporary analysis and its view of the proper role of philosophy.

The analytic movement had turned gradually to language as the clue. At this stage, many of its practitioners were convinced that ordinary language was faulty and confusing, and that if an ideal language could be invented that was clear, and, if everything we wanted to say in ordinary language could be translated into it, then we would be on the road to resolving philosophical problems. Suppose, for example, that Chinese were a perfectly clear language with no ambiguous or puzzling expressions, and that everything we wanted to say in English could be translated into Chinese. This would be a great step forward in philosophy. Of course, Chinese, like English, is a natural language, so this remark is merely for purposes of illustration. What the reductive analysts had to do was to construct an ideal language from scratch, making sure that it was free of ambiguities and ample enough to express every possible meaning.[10]

If such an ideal language could be invented, it would have the tremendous advantage of eliminating in one stroke all the obscurities and ambiguities of natural language. For instance, debates over the status of *physical objects* could be resolved if all we wanted to say about them could be translated perfectly into language about sense experiences. Then, nothing would be mysterious or puzzling about what we meant by the *material* world. If the same could be done with *mind*, then we would have one language for talking about two seemingly different *substances*. *Mind* and *matter* would be reduced to two different ways of talking about the same sense data. The redness that I perceive and the redness of an object would no longer be talked about in the puzzling mind-object vocabulary of ordinary language. The relationships could now be clarified and a centuries-old problem settled.

The new program proved to be less and less promising as the attempted translations appeared at first difficult, and then impossible. Something was always left over after the attempted translation was completed. An example of this was the proposal to get rid of

[10] Russell and Whitehead's *Principio-Mathematica* was such an attempt.

puzzles about the concept of a *nation* by translating it into language about people. For instance, the statement "England declared war" is open to the misinterpretation that a nation is a kind of fictional or metaphysical entity that can act on its own. Such an entity is a strange affair. If everything we wanted to say about such an event could be translated into language about people, then we could dispense with the fictional entity. We would not be puzzled by the question of what kind of entity a *nation* is.

Unfortunately, this translation could not be made. The number of possible human actions that would count as England declaring war is potentially enormous. A historian from Mars, for instance, who was completely ignorant of the political structure of England, might nonetheless understand perfectly the statement, "England declared war." He would not, however, have the slightest idea who did what in that event. No person or groups of persons could be considered both necessary and sufficient to such a declaration. The whole government, for instance, might have been recently killed by bombs, and a group of citizens might have done it, or the king, or a revolutionary junta, and so on. The statement "England declared war" is meaningful without the knowledge of any of these things. Therefore, it cannot be translated into language about people.

This was the fate of every effort at translation into an ideal language. Something was always left over. "Russell's success in analyzing numbers," Urmson writes, "did not show that there were really no numbers, and the failure to analyze nations into people did not show that there were nations as well as people in a metaphysically significant sense."[11] His conclusion, agreed to by most of his colleagues, was that "nothing can be reduced to anything else by philosophers, and hence there can be no philosophical successes or failures in this field."[12]

Fortunately, philosophical failures sometimes lead to promising new developments. In this case, the failure of the program of translating ordinary language into ideal language led to a new appraisal of ordinary language.

[11] Urmson, *Philosophical Analysis*, p. 183.
[12] *Ibid.*

THE TRANSITION TO ORDINARY
LANGUAGE ANALYSIS

One of the major figures in this transition was Wittgenstein who was persuaded by these failures to repudiate his earlier *Tractatus* and begin in a new way. The empiricist criterion of meaning was now gasping for breath, and reductive analysis was bogged down in failures. It became apparent to Wittgenstein that philosophers had been so hypnotized by the function of language in reporting facts (scientific language), that they had overlooked the rich manifold of meaningful uses that language demonstrates in ordinary speech.

Norman Malcolm, in his *Memoir*[13] of Wittgenstein, traces the beginning of Wittgenstein's doubts regarding the doctrines we have been discussing to an incident on a train. An Italian, who had asked him to explain his views, suddenly made a coarse gesture, flicking his hand through his beard, and said, "Now translate that!" The gesture undoubtedly had meaning, but it would plainly not fall within the categories he had been explaining.

At this moment, says Malcolm, Wittgenstein began to have serious doubts about Russell's dictum that "the essential business of language is to assert or deny facts." He observed that we are also often giving orders or obeying them, making up stories, telling jokes, asking, thanking, cursing, greeting, or praying. The meaning of these expressions would escape us if we insisted on treating them as either asserting or denying facts or as mere expressions of feeling. Instead, he noted, the important thing is to discover *how an expression is used*. As he once said, "An expression has meaning only in the stream of life."[14]

This became the dictum of the new analytic movement: Look at the language in its context; see how it is used. *Its meaning is its use*. In one of his many verbal experiments, Wittgenstein asked, "Imagine a person whose memory could not retain what the word 'pain' meant—so that he constantly called different things by that name—but nevertheless used the word in a way fitting in with the usual symptoms and presuppositions of pain—in short he uses it as

[13] Norman Malcolm, *Ludwig Wittgenstein, A Memoir* (New York: Oxford University Press, 1958).
[14] *Ibid.*, p. 93.

we all do."[15] Would he be said to know what *pain* meant? According to Wittgenstein, knowing the meaning of *pain* is knowing how to use the word properly. Or consider asking a man to define a *pawn* in chess. He might be unable to answer. If he could play chess, would we say that he did not know what *chess pawn* meant?

This latter was a favorite illustration. Wittgenstein often referred to the various moves in language as "language games." Our puzzles arise from forgetting the game we are playing, like a man who forgets he is playing chess and begins to move the pieces as checkers. "This entanglement in our rules," he wrote, "is what we want to understand (that is, get a clear view of)."[16]

This insight led Wittgenstein to revise his account of the proper function of philosophy. Its job is not to discover new *truths* about the universe, or to translate every expression into an ideal language, but to untangle the verbal web that fetters our understanding. "A main source of our failure to understand," he said, "is that we do not command a clear view of the use of our words."[17] An analytic philosopher works to reestablish the natural context of the expressions involved, "assembling" as he put it, "reminders for a particular purpose."[18] Here are more of his dicta on the subject: "A philosophical problem has the form: 'I don't know my way about.' Philosophy may in no way interfere with the actual use of language; it can in the end only describe it. . . . It leaves everything as it is."[19]

All analysts do not agree fully with Wittgenstein's way of putting the matter, but they agree that the central problems of philosophy are linguistic. If they are not the whole of philosophy, they are, as the Oxford philosopher J. L. Austin insisted, the place to begin. In his instructive essay "A Plea for Excuses," he wrote, "Certainly, then, ordinary language is not the last word: in principle it can everywhere be supplemented and improved upon and superseded. Only remember, it is the *first* word."[20]

---

[15] Ludwig Wittgenstein, *Philosophical Investigations* (New York: Macmillan, 1953), p. 95.

[16] *Ibid.*, p. 50.

[17] *Ibid.*, p. 49.

[18] *Ibid.*

[19] *Ibid.*

[20] J. L. Austin, *Philosophical Papers*, J. O. Urmson and G. J. Warnock (eds.) (New York: Oxford University Press, Inc., 1961), p. 133.

Austin's way of formulating the analytic program is less dogmatic than Wittgenstein's and invites a person who is skeptical about this way of doing philosophy to look into the clarification that analytic method might bring to his favorite themes. This is, of course, what we intend to do for education. Before applying it to educational themes, however, it will be useful to spend some time with the work of several of its distinguished practitioners. Such a review will show how different thinkers have enlarged upon the original proposal.

2

HOW ANALYSTS DO PHILOSOPHY

We have traced the process by which, during the thirty years from World War I to midcentury, ordinary language analysis evolved from the logical positivism of the Vienna Circle and the early Wittgenstein of the *Tractatus*. Now we can take a closer look at the way present-day analysts do their work. This will help us to understand how this way of doing philosophy contributes a new dimension to the philosophy of education.

Since, as we have seen, ordinary language analysis has no *truths* to convey, a sensible reason for studying this philosophy is to learn how to do it for one's self. In order to achieve proficiency, it is necessary to do more than learn the history of a school of thought or to read about what philosophers say. We must, as Wisdom says, watch them go through their antics either in person or in their publications. Thus, in spite of the fact that this book is in some ways a survey of the present state of analysis, the reader should also be initiated into the arguments themselves. This is not easy because the essence of the method shows itself only in numerous details. It is difficult to summarize arguments whose logical force lies in a patient unfolding of the numerous ways in which various problems are stated and restated. The heart of the method is precisely these subtle translations and retranslations.

A CONTRAST OF THE ANALYTIC TEMPER WITH THE CLASSICAL APPROACH

We can begin with the contrast between the classical and analytic views of reason. Blanshard says that *reason* means "the faculty and function of grasping necessary connections."[1] On the other hand, O'Connor says that *reason* means "the capacity to solve problems, of whatever kind the problem may be; or, to put the same point in another way, reason is the ability to answer questions appropriately."[2]

This difference runs deep. Classical philosophers, using *reason* as a power to grasp the real connections in nature and thought, believed themselves in possession of a tool for constructing a true picture of reality as a whole. Rejecting this as a misplaced confidence, analysts would generally agree with O'Connor that "the present state of philosophical knowledge and its past history cannot encourage us to look on philosophy as more than a *laborious piece-meal effort* to criticize and to clarify the foundations of our beliefs."[3] Philosophy cannot give us total vision. In O'Connor's words again, ". . . we cannot hope for more from philosophy than occa-

[1] Brand Blanshard, *Reason and Analysis* (La Salle, Ill.: Open Court, 1962), p. 25.
[2] D. J. O'Connor, *An Introduction to the Philosophy of Education* (London: Routledge & Kegan Paul, 1957), p. 23.
[3] *Ibid.*, p. 45.

sional and fragmentary glimpses of enlightenment along with a reasonable confidence that its continuous practice will keep our minds free of nonsense."[4] Analysis is thus not a doctrine about the world, nor much of a doctrine about philosophical method.

Classical philosophers tended to think of philosophy as a kind of superscience that integrated all the findings of the sciences, the arts, and common sense into one coherent system. But analysts argue that philosophy ceased to be a science when science broke away from philosophy in the seventeenth century, establishing its own methods and erecting its own structure of empirically verifiable knowledge. Analytic philosophers are, therefore, antimetaphysical and antispeculative in temper. The subject matter of philosophy is not the study of matters of fact (the prerogative of science), nor the study of something suprafactual (metaphysics), but simply the analysis of concepts in the context of linguistic usage. It does not attempt to tackle so-called large *mysteries* or problems of *the meaning of life*, but undertakes the prosaic chore of untangling the linguistic puzzles in which such misconceived large-scale enterprises involved us.

The analytic temper thus favors clarity over significance and is naturalistic and empirical in orientation. It also opposes what Morton White calls the existentialist way of doing philosophy, namely, in "a sprawling and turgid manner. . . ."[5] It wants, in the words of Harvard Professor Israel Scheffler, simply ". . . to clarify, improve or systematize the languages in which we express our scientific theories concerning any of a variety of subjects, as well as our common-sense beliefs, our judgments, inferences, evaluations, and convictions."[6] Among first-rate thinkers like Moore, Strawson, Wittgenstein, Wisdom, and Ryle, the results are impressive. New light is shed on many questions, and new departures for philosophical discussion are opened.

It is this piecemeal mapping of language that I want to illustrate in this chapter. In order to encompass my purpose within the scope allowed, I am going to classify the various aspects of analytic *meth-*

---

[4] *Ibid.*
[5] White, *The Age of Analysis*, p. 17.
[6] Israel Scheffler (ed.), *Philosophy and Education,* 2nd ed. (Boston: Allyn and Bacon, 1966), p. 7.

ods in a way that is apt to suggest a more doctrinaire view of method than is characteristic of analysis. Nonetheless, I believe that this is justified by a remarkable "family resemblance" among them.

SOME METHODS OF ANALYSIS

Mapping Language Categories
In his *Inaugural Lecture* at Oxford in 1945, Gilbert Ryle elaborated one of the main methods of analytical philosophy. The world of a university, he noted, contains many kinds of inquiry, each of them successful in its own way, and on its own terms. One of the chief preoccupations of the philosopher is to clarify the presuppositions or the logic of these disciplines both singly and in their relations to one another.

This clarification is possible because, as he says, "Every proposition has what can be called certain 'logical powers'; that is to say, it is related to other propositions in various discoverable logical relationships."[7] This is due to the fact that "what we label 'ideas' and 'concepts' are abstractions from the families of propositions of which they are common factors or features."[8]

He calls this task, metaphorically, "the charting of the logical power of ideas." Like the surveyor who is not content to identify the location of a single building, but who maps all the salient features of the area with all their coordinates, the philosopher seeks "to determine the cross-bearings of all of a galaxy of ideas belonging to the same or contiguous fields."[9]

Why should this task arise? One reason is that many propositions that look alike grammatically are governed by an entirely different logic. Consider, for instance, how many philosophical discussions go astray because the following sentences look alike grammatically:

1. Killing persons is punishable by law.
2. Killing persons is terrible.
3. Killing persons is morally wrong.

[7] Gilbert Ryle, *Philosophical Arguments* (New York: Oxford University Press, 1945), p. 8.
[8] *Ibid.*
[9] *Ibid.*, p. 10.

In each of these the subject, "killing persons," is qualified by a predicate. The grammar is the same, but the logic is different. Without being aware of this, one might look for the qualities "terrible" or "morally wrong" as though they performed logically like the predicate "punishable by law." In that case, we could come to know the "moral wrongness" of killing, just as we could come to know that killing is "punishable by law." But the "moral wrongness" of killing cannot be verified in this way.

John Donne once said, "Good is as visible as green." If this were so, we could verify the "moral wrongness" of killing in the same way we verify the color of something by looking at it. Many people do not agree that killing, at least of some types, is morally wrong. Are these people blind in some way analogous to color blindness?

There are two reasons why this does not seem a good way of explaining the logic of moral propositions. For instance, if a man cannot see that something is green, there are tests for his color blindness, but are there comparable tests for moral blindness? Furthermore, when a man says something is "green," we do not ask him why he thinks so. But if a man says that killing is immoral, we may properly ask him for his reasons, even if we agree with him.

We might try to get out of this difficulty by arguing that sentence 3 is more like sentence 2. In 2, we realize that the speaker is simply giving vent to his feelings about "killing persons." Perhaps, as we have seen in the last chapter, all a moral sentence does is to express a feeling about the subject under consideration. If a man says that "killing persons is terrible," we can certainly ask him why he feels that way, but the kind of reasons we expect in this case are certainly of a different sort than those we would give to assure us that "killing is punishable by law." They should also be different from those given for affirming that "killing persons is morally wrong."

What we have here, then, are three different kinds of language that look alike grammatically, but are controlled by a different logic. The philosopher's task is to map these "languages" so that a man does not get lost in this particular territory. It might help to give names to these three kinds of language. Sentence 1 is "fact-reporting" language; sentence 2 is "personal feeling" language, sentence 3 is "moral language."

The number of such "language games," as Wittgenstein called them, is very large, and it behooves us to make ourselves aware of the rules of these games. Of course, in a sense, we know the rules of these games because we use these languages correctly most of the time. That is why in the preceding examples we recognize when a mistake has been made. It is when we are led into a complicated "philosophical" use of these terms that we may become confused. Analytical philosophers relieve our confusion by reminding us of the rules that we unconsciously use correctly in familiar cases.

We know we have made a mistake when we are shown that a certain misuse of the logic of a given example leads to something odd or absurd. It is odd, for instance, to look for a quality analogous to "green," when we are trying to justify the immoral character of some act. And it is absurd to conclude a moral argument by saying, "You go on feeling your way, and I'll go on feeling my way about this matter."

Ryle calls this "confusing categories"; in this case, confusing the category *moral* with the category *color*. The rules for classifying sensory qualities like *color* are not the same as those for classifying moral properties, if, indeed, *property* is the right word here.

I have said that the number of such language games is very large. We could go on to show, for instance, that *religious* language or *aesthetic* language is significantly different from the three we have just examined. Is the statement "God exists," for instance, fact-reporting language? Is "God" a fact like, say, the planet Neptune? If so, then "God's existence" would be provable like any other fact and would be the object of some science.

Or, is "God exists" like personal preference language? Does it merely express the feelings of the speaker? Can you imagine, for instance, a believer in God agreeing that a man who denies the "existence of God" has as much right to such feelings as the believer has to his own? Does the dictum, "Concerning tastes, there is no argument" end the matter? Or, is the statement "God exists" a moral statement? If so, how would you tranlsate it into words that would reveal its moral character, making sure that nothing is left out?

To take another example, if a man says, "That painting is beautiful," is he using lanuage in any of these three ways? Is the "beauty" of the painting a fact like one of its colors or shapes? Or, is he using language in the same way as the religious believer? A closer look reveals that the logical rules for these five ways of talking are different though overlapping. Some "god-talk," for instance, does seem to move on the level of moral talk. If we say, "He is a godly man," we mean, among other things, that he is a morally good man. It would be absurd to say, "He is godly but immoral." It would also be absurd to say, "The painting is beautiful but not really good." Thus, aesthetic talk may overlap moral talk at some points.

Once it is apparent that language performs many other functions than reporting facts, it is possible to give serious attention to the logic of many different kinds of sentences. Aside from descriptive or fact-reporting sentences, analysts have identified, among others, interrogative sentences, exclamatory sentences, imperative sentences (commands), grading sentences (used in sorting out values), and performatory sentences.

These latter are interesting because they do not *refer* to anything, they *do* things. For instance, if the governor cuts a ribbon and says, "I declare this highway open," his declaration *is* the opening of the highway. Or, when the minister or priest says, "I pronounce you man and wife," his declaration accomplishes the legal union of the couple in marriage.

Distinctions like these may seem unimportant at first glance, but they are especially useful in the clarification of religious and value language. Prayer, for instance, if often performatory in character. A great deal of religious language is yet another kind of verbal behavior that can be called "celebration language." When, for instance, the priest cries out, "Great is the Lord, and greatly to be praised!" he is celebrating the greatness of God. Religious language is very complex and only recently, despite a certain diffidence, have analysts taken up the task of working with it. Wisdom's two essays, "Gods," and "The Logic of 'God'," are lucid examples of the analytic approach to this problem.[10]

---

[10] "Gods" is reprinted in his *Philosophy and Psycho-Analysis* (Blackwell, 1953). "The Logic of 'God' " was first broadcast by the British Broadcasting corporation in 1950 and first published in John Hick (ed.), *The Existence of God* (Macmillan, 1964).

Perhaps enough has been said to indicate what we mean by "mapping" the logical syntax of families of concepts, what Scheffler calls the systematic attempt to render as explicit as possible "the rules and special standards governing our valid inferences in given domains."[11] We have also, at the same time, hinted at several other methods favored by analysts. We can now look at some of them.

Category Mistakes

Implicit in the mapping process just described is the systematic classification of types of linguistic confusion that lead to mistakes. In a celebrated essay entitled "Systematically Misleading Expressions," Ryle explains the problem: "There are many expressions which occur in non-philosophical discourse which, though they are perfectly clearly understood by those who use them and those who hear or read them, are nevertheless couched in grammatical or syntatical forms which are in a demonstrable way improper to the states of affairs which they record (or the alleged states of affairs which they profess to record)."[12] By "systematically misleading," Ryle means that such an expression "naturally suggests to some people—though not to 'ordinary' people—that the state of affairs recorded is quite a different sort of state of affairs from that which it in fact is."[13]

A few examples from this essay will give the gist of its argument. The first kind of expression Ryle warns against is those that refer to the *existence* of something. For instance, "carnivorous cows do not exist" suggests by its grammatical form that there are such things as "carnivorous cows" and that they have the property of "not existing." Of course, in ordinary conversation no such mistake is ever made. The expression simply means that "no cows are carnivorous." But the "existence" form ("carnivorous cows do not exist") may be systematically misleading. Let us see why this is so. Suppose we say of a person who is now alive such things as:

---

[11] Scheffler, *Philosophy and Education*, p. 9.
[12] Gilbert Ryle, "*Systematically Misleading Expressions*," in Rorty (ed.), *The Linguistic Turn*, p. 87.
[13] *Ibid.*

Mr. White
  is a being
  is real
  is an actual object
  etc.

This has the same form as saying of an *imaginary* person such things as:

Mr. Pickwick
  is a nonentity
  is unreal
  is not a substance
  is an imaginary object
  is an idea
  etc.

As Ryle points out, none of these statements is about Mr. Pickwick, since there never was such a person. Moreover, if the first series were *false*, then it would also be true that there would not be any such person. This is odd because then the predicate ("is a being," "is a nonentity," etc.) does not have a subject to characterize as we normally expect in subject-predicate statements, such as "the grass is green." The point is that "green" and other predicates like this function in a different way than predicates asserting "existence" or "nonexistence." The way to safeguard against the puzzles that philosophers might construct from such grammatical forms is to restate such sentences in less misleading forms so that the ambiguities will not arise. For instance, "Unicorns do not exist" is clearer if we say, "nothing is *both* a quadruped *and* herbiverous *and* the wearer of one horn." Or, "carnivorous cows do not exist" could be rendered "nothing is both a cow and carnivorous."

Another example, "Satan is not a reality," suggests that it means the same kind of thing as "Capone is not a philosopher," thus apparently denying a character of a somebody called "Satan," as the latter denies a characteristic of somebody called "Capone." It would be less misleading to say " 'Satan' is not a proper name," or "No one is called 'Satan'." And, as Ryle says, "None of these statements even pretend to be about 'Satan'."[14]

The point is that *the world does not contain fictions in the way*

[14] *Ibid.*, p. 90.

that it contains historical persons, and the language used to talk about them can be systematically misleading.

Another type of systematically misleading expression meets us in such statements as "Unpunctuality is reprehensible," or "Virtue is its own reward." These appear to be similar to "Jones merits reproof" and "Smith has given himself the prize." Again the point is that "unpunctuality" and "virtue" are not things in the world in the same way that people are. In common speech, we all know this perfectly well. For instance, no one would say that virtue ought to be proud of itself. This shows that "virtue is its own reward" is not really about "virtue" at all, it is about virtuous men. Ryle concludes that in the light of this, the "age-old question of what sort of object they (virtue, etc.) are is a bogus question."[15]

For Ryle's full treatment of this theme, the reader should consult his essay, but the foregoing examples amply illustrate his method of clarifying the logical syntax of ordinary language so as to avoid the kind of misinterpretations that have confused thinkers in the past. He ends his essay with a clear statement of the analytic point of view:

> I conclude, then, that there is, after all, a sense in which we can properly inquire and even say "what it really means to say so and so." For we can ask what is the real form of the fact recorded when this is concealed or disguised and not duly exhibited in the expression in question. And we can often succeed in stating this fact in a new form of words which does exhibit what the other failed to exhibit. And I am for the present inclined to believe that this is what philosophical analysis is, and this is the sole and whole function of philosophy.[16]

The Standard of Paradigm Case

Another favored method of analysis is the standard example or so-called "paradigm case" argument. Susan Stebbing used this method to criticize a celebrated passage in Eddington's popular work *The Nature of the Physical World*. Eddington describes the atomic world of physical objects with their tiny solar systems of electrons moving about the atomic nucleus. He notes that the amount of *solid* matter in this picture is very small compared to the *empty* spaces between the particles. Then he comes to the surprising conclusion that familiar physical objects, like tabletops and wooden floors, are really like swarms of bees, not really *solid* at all. What confidence, he asks, have I that my elbow won't fall through the tabletop when I lean upon it, just like one swarm of bees flying through another?

Stebbing criticized Eddington by pointing out that the word "solid" takes its meaning from our experience with common articles like tabletops. If a tabletop is not *solid*, nothing is; the word would have no application to anything anywhere. That is to say, it is a paradigm of the concept *solid*. Eddington's illustration is therefore more misleading than enlightening. His mistake stems from a failure to understand that the logic of the concept *solid* is derived from the way we talk about ordinary objects and cannot be transferred without change to the language of science. Eddington is like a man who suddenly starts making chess moves in a game of checkers.

We will see later that the standard example works very well in trying to answer the question, "What is teaching?" We all would agree, for instance, that Socrates conversing with Meno's slave until his pupil is able to prove the famous Pythagorean hypothesis by himself is a standard (example) case of *teaching*. Starting with such an example, we can then test other examples against it. If I used Pavlovian methods to *teach* a parrot to say the words "the square of the hypotenuse is equal to the square of the other two sides," would I have *taught* the bird geometry? This seems doubtful. Certainly *teach* has been used in a very different sense than in my standard example. Or, if I repeatedly sink the eight ball in the corner pocket, would I be said to be *teaching* the eight ball to fall into the corner pocket? Certainly no one would agree to this.

This was Wittgenstein's method in his celebrated *Philosophical Investigations*. He used standard examples or paradigm cases of certain concepts and then ringed them with counter examples or border instances in such a way that the logic of the concept was gradually clarified.

The Use of Paraphrase and Translation

One of the conventions of analytic style is the use of paraphrase and translation. Articles and papers frequently contain such phrases

as "What if I were to say. . . ." Or, "Would it make sense to say.
. . ." To pick an example at random from Wittgenstein's *Philosophical Investigations*, "Would it make sense to say 'If he did
something different everyday we should not say he was obeying a
rule'?"[17] Or again, "Now someone tells me that he knows what
pain is only from his own case!"[18] Or, taking an example from education, would it make sense to say that a *trained* race horse was
"well educated"?

One of the advantages of this convention is that it is not hard
to learn, and it pays dividends in many disputes. The reason for this
is that fortunately there is usually agreement about "what we would
say if. . . ."

The Place of Special Languages

There are highly specialized languages in which this linguistic turn
is not appropriate, the language of the sciences, for instance. Here
the method is to refine and explain the concepts appropriate to the
given science systematically so as to render them, as Scheffler says,
"unambiguous, precise, and theoretically adequate." The physicists
use of *space* is an example. Ordinary language analysis is important
in instances where a scientist, who is unaware of the specialized
meaning of his words, mixes technical meanings with ordinary
usage. This, as we have seen, was Eddington's mistake in his paradox about *solidity*. *Empty space* between electrons and atomic
nuclei has a different meaning than the *empty space* between two
chairs. A good case can be made, moreover, for the proposition that
every specialized language depends ultimately upon ordinary language for its intelligibility. Technically, this is to say that ordinary
language is the *metalanguage* for every specialized language.

Austin's Method

I have said that each of the major exemplars of this way of doing
philosophy seems to have a style of his own. Moore, for instance,
attended Wittgenstein's lectures and greatly admired what he heard,
but complained that he could not do philosophy that way himself.

---

[17] Wittgenstein, *Philosophical Investigations*, p. 86.
[18] *Ibid.*, p. 100.

Austin, another celebrated figure in the movement, had his own version of the linguistic turn. Urmson, a student of Austin's, summarizes his teacher's method in this way: Having chosen some area of discourse for investigation, for instance, about responsibility, or perception or memory, we should begin by collecting "as completely as possible all the resources of the language, both idiom and vocabulary, in that area."[19] There is no rule for gathering such a collection, but there are some obvious devices: (1) free association— a kind of group brain-storming process; (2) reading relevant documents—"not the work of philosophers but, in the field of responsibility, such things as law reports, in the field of artifacts such things as mail-order catalogues";[20] and (3) reading the dictionary.

The second stage consists of "telling circumstantial stories and conducting dialogues" that "give as clear and detailed examples as possible of circumstances under which this idiom is to be preferred to that, and that to this, and of where we should (do) use this term and where that."[21] This is very like Wittgenstein's incessant story telling and imaginary dialogues. During this stage, no theorizing is allowed, because it tends to blind us to the linguistic facts of ordinary usage. When this phase is reasonably complete, we can proceed to stage three at which the results are formulated. Urmson writes: "At this stage we attempt to give general accounts of the various expressions (words, sentences, grammatical forms) under consideration; they will be correct and adequate if they make it clear why what is said in our various stories is or is not felicitous, is possible or impossible."[22]

Now we have reached a stage where we can compare these clarified ordinary usages with what "philosophers have commonly said about the expressions in question. . . ."[23] Austin's use of this method, for example in *Sense and Sensibilia*, shows how "traditional philosophical arguments depend for their apparent plausibility on the systematic misconstruction and interchange of . . . (such) key terms

[19] J. O. Urmson, "J. L. Austin," in Rorty (ed.), *The Linguistic Turn*, p. 233.

[20] *Ibid.*

[21] *Ibid.*, p. 234.

[22] *Ibid.*, pp. 234–235.

[23] *Ibid.*, p. 235.

as *illusion, delusion, hallucination, looks, appears, seems,* etc."[24]

Austin believed that with this technique, the extremely rich and subtle distinctions of ordinary language could be used to correct those "distinctions which *philosophers* thought up in their studies," and which were "very jejune and poverty-stricken by comparison with those already made in ordinary language."[25]

The Argument from Contrasting Opposites

This method is used to research the validity of a class of arguments that contain the word "all" or its equivalents. Consider the following case: Bertrand Russell once argued that in all cases of perception a person was really only seeing a portion of his own brain. He pointed out that all perception involves the stimulation of the perceiver's brain, and that no perception whatsoever takes place without such stimulation. This is, of course, a fact of physiology. From this he concluded that when a person says he is seeing a red chair he is really seeing a portion of his own brain.

Aside from the outrage to common sense that Moore noticed in this view, there is something else wrong with it. If everything is seeing one's own brain, then what would we call looking in a mirror and seeing one's brain exposed by surgery? That would seem to be what is meant by "seeing one's own brain," while looking at chairs and trees would appear to be something different. If we accept Russell's view that *all* seeing is merely seeing one's own brain, we would not have any language for talking about seeing anything else. All of our language distinctions for sense perception would disappear. On this basis, Russell could not have used the data of physiology to support his argument, because all the physiologists would have been seeing when they were studying the physiology of perception would have been their own brains. All of their elaborate accounts of the structures of the nervous system would have been merely roundabout ways of talking about their own brains.

The point of this argument is that for the phrase "looking at our own brain" to have meaning it must contrast with something that is not a case of "looking at one's own brain."

---

24 *Ibid.*
25 *Ibid.*

Consider another instance in which contrasts are wiped out and the meaning of an assertion is again rendered empty. John Wisdom in his essay entitled "Gods" tells a parable which has become famous in analytic literature. Cited is Antony Flew's version of the parable because it is briefer than the original:

> Once upon a time two explorers came upon a clearing in the jungle. In the clearing were growing many flowers and many weeds. One explorer says, "Some gardener must tend this plot." The other disagrees, "There is no gardener." So they pitch their tents and set a watch. No gardener is ever seen. "But perhaps he is an invisible gardener." So they set up barbed-wire fence. They electrify it. They patrol with bloodhounds. . . . But no shrieks ever suggest that some intruder has received a shock. No movements of the wire ever betray an invisible climber. The bloodhounds never give cry. Yet still the Believer is not convinced. "But there is a gardener who has no scent and makes no sound, a gardener who comes secretly to look after the garden which he loves."[26]

Now Flew draws his conclusion: "At last the Sceptic despairs, 'But what remains of your original assertion? Just how does what you call an invisible, intangible, eternally elusive gardener differ from an imaginary gardener or even from no gardener at all?' " This is what Flew calls "the death by a thousand qualifications."[27] If there is no way to distinguish between a garden tended by a gardener and one not tended by a gardener, all talk of a gardener is meaningless. As Flew says, ". . . if there is nothing which a putative assertion denies then there is nothing which it asserts either: and so it is not really an assertion."[28] In other words, unless some contrasting of affairs can at least be imagined the affirmation of a given state of affairs has no real meaning.

This argument is effective against many types of *all* statements. For instance, if *all* my experience is alleged to be illusory (as in Descartes' discussion of a "universal deceiver"), then there is no meaning to saying that any part of it is illusory. *Illusory* must contrast with something nonillusory. Or, if everything is *mind*, there is

---

[26] Antony Flew, "Theology and Falsification," in *New Essays in Philosophical Theology*, Antony Flew and Alasdair MacIntyre (eds.) (London: SCM Press, 1955), p. 96.

[27] *Ibid.*, p. 97.

[28] *Ibid.*, p. 98.

no way of contrasting things that are *mind* with things that are not mind, and the general statement loses significance.

Wisdom is not prepared to accept the term "meaningless" for such proposals, but he does agree that they cannot be confirmed empirically or experimentally. In such cases, we would be wise to notice that language is being used in some other way than the reporting of facts.

CRITICISM AND DEFENSE OF ANALYTIC METHOD

Now that we have sampled the ways in which analysts do philosophy, let us look at their defense of these methods. Critics often ask, "Why should we pay so much attention to ordinary language?" In his essay "A Plea for Excuses," Austin replies to this query: ". . . our common stock of words embodies all the distinctions men have found worth drawing, and the connexions they have found worth making, in the lifetimes of many generations: these surely are likely to be more numerous, more sound, since they have stood up to the long test of the survival of the fittest, and more subtle, at least in all ordinary and reasonable practical matters, than any that you or I are likely to think up in our armchairs of an afternoon— the most favoured alternative method."[29]

Richard Rorty adds another point on behalf on ordinary language: ". . . philosophers who disagree about everything else can agree on how they use words in non-philosophical discourse."[30] This is no small consideration in the light of the potential bearing of such agreement on philosophical disputes.

The value of an appeal to ordinary language is like a comment once made by the satirical columnist Arthur Hoppe when he was asked how he got his ideas. "I read through the paper," he said, "until I come to an item that I don't understand—then I explain it to everybody." The speculative philosopher seems to look at life until he finds something he cannot understand, and then he explains it to everybody, but the explanation is often impossible to

[29] Austin, *Philosophical Papers*, p. 130.
[30] Rorty (ed.), *The Linguistic Turn*, p. 19.

understand. The analytic philosopher, by contrast, reads through philosophy until he finds things that philosophers have puzzled over without success and then explains them in language that everyone understands.

To what does the demand for a *justification* of analysis amount? Is the critic asking for some final proof, some certainty that is impervious to all doubt? If you look at the ways in which the word "justification" is used in various contexts, you will see that *justification* is never used in this absolute sense.[31]

Stuart Hampshire in his defense of ordinary language goes further than this: "We cannot step outside the language which we use, and judge it from some ulterior and superior vantage-point."[32] Burtt gives further force to this remark by noting that "thinking always occurs in a linguistic framework that is social. . . ."[33] Language has evolved in the culture in which a person chooses to talk. He cannot control the meaning of his words. They have taken their meaning from the style or "form of life" that characterizes that culture.

If all this sounds dogmatic, Rorty shows how the question can be thrown back to the critic.

If . . . you think that there are questions which common sense and science cannot answer, it is up to you not just to state them, but to show how they *can* be answered. If you think that there is more to be described and explained than is described in, or explained by common sense and science, tell us how you know whether you have described it accurately, or have explained it correctly. If you cannot do either of these things, then we shall persist in regarding your questions . . . as bad questions."[34]

Another question often asked by critics is this: How do you know when you have a good analysis? By what criteria can you judge that your analysis is complete? This is similar to the question that used to be put to pragmatists: How do you know when a problem is solved? In neither case is the answer a logical one, but a practical

[31] E. A. Burtt, *In Search of Philosophical Understanding* (New York: New American Library, 1965), p. 49.
[32] Stuart Hampshire, "Identification and Existence," in *Contemporary British Philosophy*, H. D. Lewis (ed.), (London: Macmillan, 1956), p. 192.
[33] Burtt, *In Search of Philosophical Understanding*, p. 50.
[34] Rorty (ed.), *The Linguistic Turn*, p. 14.

one. You know when your puzzle has given way to clarity, when you see your way about, when you are no longer baffled by your experience.

This is very like asking a psychiatrist when he knows that his patient is no longer in need of therapy. The answer is that he no longer needs therapy when he is able to make his way in the common world of men without the crippling effects of his previous befuddlements. Therefore, it is not surprising that Wittgenstein had recourse to the analogy of psychoanalysis in referring to the services of philosophy. In the long run, no doubt, men will continue to use a method that gives them clarification and reduces the puzzles that impede their thought even though they have no theoretically complete and final *justification* of the method itself.

Another challenge to analysts is why a philosopher should concern himself with words rather than experiences. In general, I suppose, analysts would reply that science alone is equipped to handle empirical matters with methods that have been refined through successful use. If philosophers dealt with experience, they would become mere amateur scientists with no real standing. Austin's reply to this question, on the other hand, is not so restrictive. He writes: "When we examine what we should say when, what words we should use in what situations, we are looking again not *merely* at words but also at the realities we use the words to talk about. . . ."[35] He even suggested that perhaps we should give this philosophy some less misleading name. His suggestion, "linguistic phenomenology."[36] Then he added, that is "rather a mouthful."

Future Directions

Austin's remarks suggests that, in the future, analysts may find themselves working at problems in a way that intersects the interests of European phenomenology and even the existentialism that they so often criticize. Many of the commonsense ways in which I have characterized analysis exclude some of the new things that analysts do, and even some things that their most celebrated exemplars have done for some time. Oxford professor P. F. Strawson,

[35] Austin, *Philosophical Papers*, p. 130.
[36] *Ibid.*

for instance, has worked at what he calls "descriptive metaphysics," a search for basic categories of language that control everything we can say. His enterprise looks surprisingly like the work of the classical philosophers. *The Bounds of Sense,* for instance, is a linguistic approach to many of the same critical problems with which Kant worked. Wisdom's writings are also hard to force into the strict characterization I have drawn.

By now, the major outlines of analytic procedure should be clear enough to turn to the question of how this way of doing philosophy bears on education.

3

ANALYTICAL PHILOSOPHY OF
EDUCATION

Philosophy of education is broadly speaking a philosophical study of education. Since the nature of this enterprise depends heavily upon how one views the task of philosophy, let us begin by contrasting analytic philosophy of education with alternative conceptions.

What passes as philosophy of education among many educators is comparable to what one would speak of colloquially as one's "philosophy of life," with special reference to education. This normally consists of a collection of wise sayings about the nature of reality, one's ideals and expectations, and a general view about what makes the educational enterprise work in a worthwhile way. By the latter, I mean such things as techniques for successful teaching, and ideas of school organization and administration with some notions of community relationships. All this is, no doubt, valuable in its own way, but it has little to do with the analytical philosophy of education. Philosophy of an analytic stripe has nothing to do with solving factual questions, such as the best way to teach languages, for example. Nor are philosophers necessarily gifted in their sensitivity to ideals or values. Nor do they possess any special sagacity in practical affairs or personality problems. Their metier is the *logic* of whatever claims may be made about any of these subjects. The philosopher's business, writes Corbett, "is with the principles of valid thought that underlie all particular issues."[1] Given a technique of teaching, the philosopher can analyze the concepts involved and the logic of their interrelationships. But they have no philosophical means for prophesying the consequences of proposed methods or techniques. "Discussion of all these questions," writes O'Connor, "are of course, interesting and valuable to students of education but it is a pity to suggest that they are philosophical."[2]

In truth, if you turn to the great names in the history of philosophy who have written on education—say to Plato's *Republic* or Whitehead's *Aims of Education*—you will discover persuasive and even wise discourses on all of these things. The fact that these remarks about education are the work of philosophers who happen also to be wise human beings does not necessarily qualify them as philosophy of education. Such a philosophy of education, writes the English philosopher Edward Best, "is only a theory of education masquerading under a fancy name, and one cannot but suspect that many of those who freely use this phrase mean only the educational theories of people with a historical reputation as philosophers."[3] *Theory of education*, it should be noted, is not the same thing as *philosophy of education*.

Another approach to the philosophy of education is a by-product of the traditional way of doing philosophy. Many textbooks in the

[1] J. P. Corbett, "Teaching Philosophy Now," in Reginald D. Archambault (ed.), *Philosophical Analysis and Education* (New York: Humanities Press, 1965), p. 142.

[2] O'Connor, *An Introduction to the Philosophy of Education*, p. 14.

[3] Edward Best, "Common Confusions in Educational Theory," in Archambault (ed.), *Philosophical Analysis and Education*, p. 49.

subject begin by expounding the world views of selected philosophical schools and then deduce from these philosophies certain conclusions about education. Each school's views about human nature,
the world, knowledge, values, society, and so on, are set forth, and
then the educational significance of these respective doctrines is
expounded. In this way, educators are expected to gain some wisdom about their own tasks from the accumulated wisdom of philosophy.

This pattern will not work with analytic philosophy since
analysts initially deny that there are any philosophical "truths"
about the universe and man. Furthermore, analytic philosophers
point out, with this procedure the educator is still left with a collection of so-called truths, some of which are contradicted by the
others. How then is he to choose wisely without any criterion of
choice except his own personal unphilosophical preferences. It
would be quite different if philosophers could agree upon a world
view that is the truest, for then there would be solid ground for
educational implications. Lacking such agreement, say the analysts,
we must attack the problem in another way.

What analytic philosophers propose to do in the field of education is not to start with certain philosophical *truths*, but to go
directly to the concepts that are central to the rich field of educational theory and practice. Here they find ample grist for their
analytic mill. Scheffler states the point of view clearly. Philosophy,
he says, "aims explicitly at improving our understanding of education by clarification of our conceptual apparatus—the ways in which
we formulate our beliefs, arguments, assumptions, and judgments
concerning such topics as learning and teaching, character and
intellect, subject-matter and skill, desirable and appropriate means
of schooling."[4]

The question still lingers: Is this all there is to the philosophy
of education? Many analytic philosophers would say emphatically
that it is. Others who have found the analytic approach valuable
insist that this is not the whole story, that analysis can be combined with more traditional ways of doing philosophy. For instance,
William K. Frankena of the University of Michigan holds that the

---

[4] Scheffler, *Philosophy and Education*, p. 4.

"complete philosopher" will not only analyze in the ways we have described, but he will also speculate about the world as a whole and philosophize about goals, norms, and standards of human existence, hopefully yielding some "guide to human action." This latter enterprise, joined to a philosophical analysis of moral terms (such as *right* and *good*), he claims to be the "heart of the philosophy of education." Much of the material for this kind of philosophizing, he says, will be taken from factual materials of the sciences and common sense.[5] This is a theme worth exploring, but it is not the purpose of this work. By staying close to a stricter methodology, it will be easier to see just where the issues lie between analytic and other ways of doing philosophy.

Several of the most celebrated contemporary analysts, like Strawson and Wisdom, have opened the door to wider speculation, leaving the possibility that analysis may someday move in this direction. Wisdom, for example, finds viable meaning in some metaphysical systems. His point is that a metaphysical system, though not verifiable in its entirety, may serve a useful purpose. It may enable us to see certain aspects of experience that would not have been otherwise visible. For example (this is not his illustration), pragmatism may enable us to perceive the degree to which our concepts are instruments for problem solving and to think of *intelligence* as the power to reconstruct experience. Before the advent of pragmatism, this could easily have been overlooked. Marxism helps us to see that much of our social philosophy is class oriented. Idealism points up the degree to which our experience is a mental construction, and materialism enables us to get a fuller view of the degree to which life is understandable as material process. Existentialism focuses on the individual in his uniqueness and his freedom. For Wisdom, such metaphysical schemes are quasi-poetic devices for improving our vision. In this sense, we may appreciate analytically, at least in some measure, the older way of doing the philosophy of education by the route of metaphysical systems. The fact remains that the essential job of philosophy as such is understood as analysis, not speculation.

To sum up: An analytic philosophy of education will consist in

[5] William K. Frankena, "Toward a Philosophy of the Philosophy of Education," *Harvard Education Review*, 26, no. 2 (Spring 1956), p. 97.

an analysis of educational concepts both singly and in relation to one another. I mean, attempts to answer such questions as: What are teaching, learning, and education? What is the meaning of *authority* in education? What is the relationship between the concept of *excellence* and the concept of *equality* in a *democratic* educational system? What is *moral* education? And so on.

How Useful Is Analytic Philosophy to Education

This question has already been answered in a general way, but let us take it a bit further. We have seen that philosophy is not an empirical enterprise and therefore cannot take the place of educational research, nor supply answers to factual questions. Nor, for that reason, can it take the place of advancing concrete solutions to practical problems. It can, however, make educational research more successful by clarifying the concepts used in research, analysing the terms of problems, distinguishing types of problems, and clarifying the categories of language appropriate to them. It can also aid in the interpretation of results of research so that these results are not misapplied to educational issues because of conceptual confusions.

There is, for example, a great deal of research on so-called learning theory that lacks any clear notion of what it means to *learn*. The results of such research are often taken over by educators as solutions to educational problems without digesting the conceptual context in which the terms of the research were used. This gives the appearance of being a scientific approach to educational problems, but it is, in fact, very misleading. When the problems concerning the concept of learning are taken up in a later chapter, this point will be made clearer.

I have said that philosophy cannot be substituted for advancing concrete solutions to practical problems. Such solutions, when they are viable, are a mixture of philosophical clarity, educational theory, practical good sense, and scientific expertise. Nor can philosophy be substituted for educational policy making. Educational policy is a very complex affair. The educator is a man who must make decisions and who, therefore, must take risks that cannot be eliminated by either empirical knowledge or logical acumen. Education, like medicine, includes not only scientific knowledge, but moral judgments, and, of course, the risks and uncertainties of existence that surround us on all sides. Education is oriented to practical activity. As Paul Hirst says, "Education being the kind of activity it is, the theory must range right across and be drawn from many kinds of knowledge, value judgments and beliefs including the metaphysical, the epistemological and the religious."[6] This has a bearing on the nature of policy making. To quote Hirst again: "It is difficult to see how conclusions that depend on the putting together of considerations from practical experience, from psychology, social theory and philosophy, weighing them up, estimating their relative importance, could possibly be reached in an uninterrupted chain of deduction."[7]

Let me cite a nonanalytic philosopher, Louis Arnaud Reid, on this same important point: "Thought," he writes, "is shaped, and grows, in a living context of value-feelings and judgments; and the end-product, the educational judgment, is really much more the outcome of what I may perhaps be allowed to call 'sensitive principled global thinking' than of cold logic."[8]

It is precisely because educational judgments are built upon materials drawn from so many different sources that philosophical skill is needed to avoid misuse of the materials. "In such a complex activity," writes Hirst, "serious problems of meaning frequently occur and in particular a failure to understand the relations between different fields of discourse befogs many educational issues."[9] For instance, it is important to know the difference between the logic of concepts drawn from different regions of the diverse study we call psychology, especially the difference between concepts in clinical psychology and experimental psychology, and, in the former, the multiplicity of clinical theories makes the task even more urgent. Or again, we should know the difference between the logic of moral or value judgments and empirical judgments. It is in this light that Hirst proposes his definition of philosophy of education: "The term 'philosophy of education' is perhaps best used," he writes, "to

[6] Paul Hirst, "Philosophy and Educational Theory," in Scheffler (ed.), *Philosophy and Education*, p. 90.

[7] *Ibid.*, p. 82.

[8] Louis Arnaud Reid, "Philosophy and the Theory and Practice of Education," in Archambault (ed.), *Philosophical Analysis and Education*, p. 29.

[9] *Ibid.*, p. 92.

refer to the comprehensive contribution of distinctively philosophical methods of investigation to the discussion of problems that occur within the educational theory."[10]

Another area in which analytic philosophy can be of help is in the sphere of values and moral education. This may seem to be a strange claim, since the empirical tradition has, on the whole, not been very helpful in this field. The emotive theory of value which resulted from a strict application of the verifiability theory of meaning did in fact remove judgments of value from the realm of rationality altogether. But much has happened since the publication of Ayer's *Language Truth and Logic*. Scheffler has these new developments in mind when he writes: "The word has gone out, it seems, that ethical and moral questions are beyond the reach of rational discussion. As a result, dogmatic appeals to commitment multiply and persuasive rhetoric replaces argument, short-circuiting the deliberative process, frustrating the demands for reasons, and stilling the critical impulse."[11]

A skeptical viewpoint has been nourished by the social sciences in which the student is deluged by a welter of contradictory styles of personal and social life. In a day when education is threatened by ideologies and dogmatisms of all kinds and is itself uncertain of its directions or even of the value of its essential services, a chartless skepticism is bound to prevent any vigorous coming to grips with the necessities of reconstituting the educational enterprise on defensible grounds.

In recent years, contemporary analytic philosophy has begun the task of clarifying the distinctive concepts in the realm of discourse we call morality. We now have much better understanding of the function of such terms as *ought, right, desirable, worthwhile,* and *good,* and the distinctive procedures for answering questions that are raised in the moral realm. We will be looking into this matter later.

To summarize the value of analysis to education, I should say that the chief value lies in whatever value clarity has for any enterprise whatsoever. To be clear about one's thought in any practical

[10] *Ibid.,* p. 94.

[11] Israel Scheffler, preface to R. S. Peters, *Ethics and Education* (Chicago: Scott, Foresman, 1966).

matter is to turn on a light and be able to see. For those who would rather function in the twilight of feeling and persuasive rhetoric, such a value is, of course, not very weighty. One can only hope that their number will diminish. The habit of clarity, asking what one means at each stage of thought, is not a natural virtue. It is won only by the most persistent discipline, and it has had only variable success since its first martyr in Socrates. But to those who have had a glimpse of its possibilities, it suggests a new dimension in the civilizing of our humanity.

A MAPPING OF PHILOSOPHY OF EDUCATION

One of the tasks of philosophy is mapping the logic of some region of discourse, laying it out, so to speak, so that a person can make his way about it successfully. In my opinion, one useful job of mapping has been done by Frankena in his book *Philosophy of Education.*[12] I summarize it here as an illustration of the service that philosophy can render to the clarification of our discourse about education.

The essence of Frankena's map lies in the following diagram:

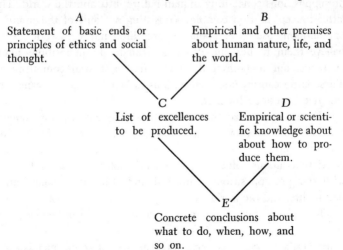

A
Statement of basic ends or principles of ethics and social thought.

B
Empirical and other premises about human nature, life, and the world.

C
List of excellences to be produced.

D
Empirical or scientific knowledge about about how to produce them.

E
Concrete conclusions about what to do, when, how, and so on.

[12] William K. Frankena (ed.), *Introduction to Philosophy of Education* (New York: Macmillan, 1965).

"Education," Frankena has written, "is the process by which society makes of its members what it is desirable that they should become . . . either in general or in so far as this may be carried on by what are called 'schools.' "[13] With this as a frame of reference, he sorts out the desired levels of knowledge that function as our guides to decision making in practical educational affairs. Conclusions at E (judgments about what to do) are a mixture of judgments about the "excellences to be produced" (C) in the beneficiaries of the educational process, combined with "empirical or scientific knowledge about how to produce them" (D). It is important to notice that we cannot derive the list of prescriptions, excellencies, that are a set of value judgments about what to do, from the descriptive, empirical, knowledge accounts of what the facts actually are. It is, in short, not possible to go directly from scientific understanding to policy and practice. Practice is always a combination of prescriptive convictions and descriptive understanding.

Going back up the ladder, we can see that C, the list of excellencies, is itself a judgment based upon a judicious combination of A, our presuppositions of the basic ends of life and the fundamental principles of right action and right social organization, and B, our presuppositions concerning human nature, life, and the world. This latter concept is itself complex, consisting not only of the empirical or commonsense facts about nature, life, and the world as we believe them to be, but also our ultimate presuppositions about existence, our metaphysical beliefs, and existential commitments. These latter can include such notions as belief in God or a naturalistic rejection of such belief.

We can summarize this ladder by saying that E, our concrete conclusion about what to do, presupposes judgments about values (C) and empirical claims (D). C in turn presupposes our ultimate convictions about values and moral principles (A) in combination with our presuppositions, empirical and otherwise, about human nature, life, and the world.

The analysis of our activities as educators, then, can be made clear

[13] William K. Frankena, "Toward a Philosophy of the Philosophy of Education," p. 95.

only when we have spelled out these various elements presupposed by our activities. Socrates' celebrated dictum that the unexamined life is not worth living can be paraphrased for the educator: Unexamined educating is not worth doing.

Why not? The question almost seems not worth asking since it would seem that any person engaged in an activity in which he believes would want to know just what he was *really* about. I suppose most people would say that they do prefer to know. But, in fact, very few, as Socrates discovered to his dismay, really do know or really bother to undertake the inquiry necessary to know what they are about.

There are many values in being clear what one is about. One is that it may turn out upon examination not to be what one *really* wants to do. Life can be frustrating to the man who gives himself to one activity after another only to discover that he has not been doing what he intended. To examine educational activities may alter them in many ways toward a more desirable type of behavior.

A second value of being clear is that it enables men of goodwill to enter into rational discussion about their practices. Such a dialogue is bound to improve the amount of wisdom and knowledge that goes into education.

A third value is that such examination will reveal unconscious errors in deducing lower levels in the chart from the higher ones. The move from basic ends and ethical principles, to lists of excellences, to concrete conclusions, is, as I have pointed out, a hazardous process. It is difficult at best, and when done unconsciously—that is to say thoughtlessly—it is subject to many more hazards. To believe, for example, in democratic principles about social life is one thing, but to use them logically as a guide to specific excellencies and to specific educational practices is another. This can only be done well in the full light of consciousness, and we know that clarification is never finished. New light is always dawning on the meaning of concepts at every level, with the consequence that the whole enterprise has to be forever reexamined.

All of this is even more evident in an era when almost every item in each category is challenged by events and by new interpretations. The only hope of making our way creatively through such an era is to become more philosophical. This does not mean that philosophers can do the whole job. It means that educators must learn to do philosophy—no doubt with the aid of philosophers—and to take this task to heart so that they can benefit from the light of reason in so far as that light can guide our lives.

PART II
THE ANALYSIS OF CONCEPTS
RELEVANT TO EDUCATION

4

TEACHING

Now that we have laid the foundation for understanding philosophical analysis with its historical and methodological background, it should not be too difficult to follow an analysis of basic concepts of education. We will begin with three of the most important concepts: *teaching, learning,* and *educating,* along with such satellite concepts as *training, conditioning, instructing,* and *indoctrinating.* Covered in a later chapter will be the concepts central to proposals made to teachers on how they should go about their task: *behavioral outcomes, relevance, readiness,* and *learning to learn.* We will then consider concepts that come out of curricular discussions. Another important area of examination will be the place of *values* in education. A final chapter will analyze the concept of *democracy* and its bearing on education. All of this is merely a sampling, an important sampling, for as R. S. Peters has pointed out, there are enough concepts in education awaiting analytic clarification to keep philosophers busy for the next half-century.

WHAT IS A CONCEPT?

Since the word "concept" is used so frequently, it is important to understand what is meant by it. A concept, such as *teaching*, for example, is an abstraction from the interrelated body of propositions in which it naturally occurs. By looking closely at the way this concept is used in its natural setting, we can discover its logical powers, the way it work linguistically, and separate it out from concepts that are similar in some ways, but distinct enough to be regarded as significantly different. *Counseling* or *preaching*, for instance, are in many ways like *teaching*, but their logical performance is different enough to be distinguished from it. Conversely, other concepts, like *instructing*, are closely related to *teaching*. These relationships can be diagrammed or mapped, somewhat like relatives in a family tree.

Thomas Green tell us that "a concept is a rule." "When someone learns a concept," he writes, "without exception, what he has learned is a rule, a rule of language, or more generally, a rule of behavior."[1] When we learn the meaning of *teach*, we have learned the rule or rules that guide the correct usage of the word. This does not mean that we, or perhaps anyone, can state the rule. Rules of speech are often very complicated. When we analyze our usage, however, we rely upon our implicit understanding of such rules, and progressively bring to light some of the logical dimensions of the term.

Paul Komisar and Thomas Nelson suggest that a "conceptual analysis of teaching should culminate (simply) in a definition of

---

[1] Thomas F. Green, "A Topology of the Teaching Concept," in J. C. B. Macmillan and Thomas W. Nelson (eds.), *Concepts of Teaching: Philosophical Essays* (Skokie, Ill.: Rand McNalley, 1968), p. 28.

the term teaching."[2] This way of saying it distinguishes conceptual analysis from the attempt to say what teaching *ought* to be, or from proposing some special program of teaching as the model for teaching as such.[3] These later efforts are useful in their own way, but they are not conceptual analysis. Komisar and Nelson point out, "Unfortunately, in most educational jargon a concept of something (for example, readiness or education) includes not only a statement of the meaning of the term (readiness, education), but also bits of facts, anecdotes (sometimes called 'theories'), and even value judgments regarding the actual phenomena."[4]

It would be a mistake to suppose that the logical boundaries of the concept of *teaching* can be clearly marked. The rules that govern its use are numerous and sometimes ambiguous, but this does not prevent our being able to mark out with considerable clarity some of the main features of the term so as to distinguish it from terms that are quite different. Also, it does not prevent us from seeing the relationship of *teaching* to *telling* or *indoctrinating*. For example, when the edges of a red patch in a painting are blurred, we are not prevented from seeing the red patch in relation to its surroundings, and distinguishing it decisively from a neighboring blue patch.

Now let us begin the mapping of what we mean by *teaching*.

THE TEACHING CONTINUUM

Thomas F. Green, in his essay "A Topology of the Teaching Concept,"[5] diagrams teaching and its satellite notions in the following

[2] Paul Komisar and Thomas Nelson, "Introduction: Conceptual Analysis of Teaching," in Macmillan and Nelson (eds.), *Concepts of Teaching: Philosophical Essays*, p. 92.

[3] See Israel Scheffler, *The Language of Education* (Springfield, Ill.: Charles C Thomas, 1960), Chapter One.

[4] Komisar and Nelson, "Introduction: Conceptual Analysis of Teaching," in Macmillan and Nelson (eds.), *Concepts of Teaching: Philosophical Essays*, p. 92.

[5] Green, "A Topology of the Teaching Concept," in Macmillan and Nelson (eds.), *Concepts of Teaching: Philosophical Essays*, p. 36.

way. By keeping this diagram in mind, it will be easier to place these notions in logical relationship to one another

Behavior, Conduct		Knowledge, Beliefs	
Intimidation	Training	Instructing	Propagandizing
Physical Threat	Conditioning	Indoctrinating	Lying

The Region of Intelligence

Teaching aims, on the one hand, at changes in behavior and conduct, or, on the other hand, at the acquisition of new knowledge or beliefs. *Training* is clearly an effort to change behavior, while *instructing* aims at the acquisition of knowledge or beliefs. The fact that *training* often includes instruction, and that instruction may be supportive of some aspect of a training program, should not obscure the logical differences between these two aspects of the teaching concept. *Conditioning* belongs on the behavior side of the diagram, to the left of *training*, because it appeals less to intelligence than to training. When we come to *intimidation* or *physical threat*, we have moved outside of the region of intelligence, although such methods are sometimes used to affect changes in behavior. We shall see why intimidation and physical threat lie outside the boundaries of *teaching* as such.

On the right side of the diagram, *indoctrinating* is a kind of *instructing*, but it appeals less (as we shall see) to intelligence, and therefore is to the right of *instructing*, moving to the edge of the region of intelligence. *Propagandizing* and *lying* are beyond appeals to intelligence, and therefore, like physical threat, are outside the pale of *teaching*. Other related concepts can be put on the diagram as we proceed.

Unlike swimming, or playing tennis, you cannot tell from simply watching a person's behavior whether or not he is teaching. The teacher may be talking or silent, sitting, standing on his head, moving, or resting. Thus, teaching is not a specific set of activities. To know whether a person is teaching, we have to judge his behavior by a relevant standard or criterion. I shall argue that the proper criterion of whether a person's activities are *teaching*, depends upon whether he is intentionally trying to bring about in another person some kind of understanding, coupled with a disposition to use that understanding in appropriate ways.

On the other hand, no one can teach without doing *something*. "What were you doing?" "I was teaching." "Yes, I know, but what specifically were you doing?" "I was just teaching, that is all." "But were you lecturing?" "No, as a matter of fact I was listening to a recitation." To teach, then, means to do something, but that something must satisfy the above criterion.

Let us turn our illustrative conversation around. "What were you doing?" "I was leading a discussion." "Oh, you were teaching." "No, it was a group counseling session." No doubt, teachers sometimes counsel, but in this they are not necessarily teaching. How does counseling differ from teaching, since many of the activities of counselors are similar to those of teachers? They differ from one another by the criterion of their success. A counselor's aim is different from that of a teacher. This aim or standard defines his behavior, just as the criterion of educating defines the activity of the teacher.

The teacher does many things: keeps order, sends sick children to the school nurse, counsels an upset child, turns up the heat, or opens a window. Our problem can be put schematically:

Doctoring (medical) is to medical care
And counseling is to psychological therapy
As teaching is to X

Our question is, "What is X?" Peters answers this question as follows: "If we look at such a process from the teacher's point of view he is intentionally trying to get learning processes going by exhibiting, drawing attention to, emphasizing, or explicating some fraction of what has to be learnt or putting the learner in a position where his experience is likely to become structured along desirable lines."[6]

The teacher is not teaching when he opens the window, polices students, or supervises the school lunchroom. If the room is disorderly, too hot, or the children hungry, then learning is unlikely

[6] R. S. Peters (ed.), *The Concept of Education* (London: Routledge & Kegan Paul, 1967), p. 9.

to go on. These activities sustain teaching, but they are not themselves teaching.

TEACHING IS TRIADIC

Teaching involves three elements: a teacher, a subject matter, and a student. "What were you doing this afternoon?" "I was teaching." "What were you teaching?" "Oh, nothing at all, just teaching." This does not make sense. To teach means to teach something, a subject matter.

"You say you were teaching." "Yes." "Whom were you teaching?" "No one, just teaching by myself." "You mean you were teaching yourself?" "No, I wasn't teaching anyone, not even myself." This does not make sense either.

One of the ways to clarify the concept of *teaching* is to agree on a standard example, what philosophers call a "paradigm case." The following incident from one of Plato's dialogues is a good candidate for such a paradigm. In the *Meno*, Socrates illustrates one of his favorite doctrines by teaching one of Meno's slaves a concept in geometry. Socrates does not *tell* the slave about the Pythagorean theorem concerning the square of the hypotenuse. Socrates asks him questions, beginning with things he already knows, such as that a square has four equal lines, and so on. Gradually, he works up to the more complex notion of triangles with squares built along their sides, until the slave is able to draw the conclusion that the square of the hypotenuse of a right angle is equal in area to the sum of the square of the other two sides. It is hard to imagine someone questioning whether this is teaching or not.

This is a logical model of *teaching*. The elements are all here: A teacher who understands enough to lead the inquiry, a subject matter, and a potential learner.

TEACHING AS A "TASK" WORD

Suppose Socrates had failed in his instruction, would we say that he had not been teaching? I think not. Teaching intends to bring about learning, but sometimes it does not. If the teacher does not intend to bring about learning, he is not teaching. If he intends learning, he can still claim to have been teaching even though he fails. One way of making this point is to say that teaching is a *task* word rather than an *achievement* word. Communication, for instance, is an *achievement word*. You cannot *communicate* without getting some message through to another person. *Fishing,* on the other hand, like teaching, is a *task* word. A man may fish without catching anything. However, as James Gribble points out, "if no one had ever caught fish by dangling baited line into the water it would not be called fishing. Verbs only develop a *task* sense if an activity is sometimes successful."[7] This suggests that with any specific activity that claims to be *teaching* it is necessary to establish that there is some chance of learning being generated. This leaves the status of any specific so-called *teaching* method open to inquiry.

The claim that some form of activity is properly designated a *teaching method* is also subject to other criteria than potential success. Learning can, no doubt, be brought about through threats and intimidation, but this would not normally be called *teaching*. The reason is that *teaching* in its paradigmatic sense belongs to the sphere of intelligence, and these methods make little or no appeal to the understanding or intellect of the learner. If we saw someone beating a child, we might agree that the child was learning something, but we would hardly credit the beating as *teaching*. Here again, the lines are not clear. Threats and rewards are sometimes used in teaching. It is only in extreme forms that we would categorically refuse to count them as teaching. These boundaries become clearer when we examine some related concepts.

TRAINING

Compare the Socratic model with the following: You teach your dog to jump through a hoop, or your parrot to say, "Thank you." The three standard elements are again present: a teacher, a subject

---

[7] James Gribble, *Introduction to Philosophy of Education* (Boston: Allyn & Bacon, 1969), p. 5.

matter, and a potential learner, but the element of understanding is missing. Despite the fact that it would be correct to speak of "teaching your dog tricks," ordinary speech still recognizes a difference. We would not, for instance, say that your dog or parrot were "well educated." We would say that they are "well trained." If you *taught* a computer to play chess, we would not say that the computer was "trained," much less "educated" to play chess. Nor would we say that the computer "understood" chess.

Ordinary language often makes no distinction between training and teaching. "I taught him to swim," and "I trained him to swim," are both correct usage. It is only in more complex situations that our speech makes the distinctions that are useful for clarifying the full meaning of *teaching* as distinct from *training*.

Even in complex subject matters like medicine, law, or education, we speak of *training*: medical *training*, legal *training*, or teacher *training*. The expressions "medical education" or "legal education" are not quite right. When we use these latter expressions we imply something more than training. When we talk about the "education of doctors" or "the education of teachers," we mean something more than the *training* of doctors or teachers. We are concerned with their nonprofessional backgrounds. One of the issues in the education of teachers lies precisely in the difference betwen narrow professional *training* and a broad *education*. One would not say, "My education is in medicine/law/the ministry/teaching." We would say, "My training is in medicine, etc." This is true also of learning other subject matter: history, literature, or languages. You would not say, "My education is in history." You would say, "My training is in history."

Throughout the preceding examples, the notion of *education* is broader than that of *training*. In a later chapter, we shall see in more detail what the concept of *education* involves. For the present, it is enough to indicate that it is closely related to certain central notions of *teaching*. Education involves, as does the paradigmatic sense of *teaching*, the notion of understanding rather than the mere acquisition of specific skills or limited bodies of knowledge.

It would be wrong to deny that *training* is a kind of teaching. It lies within the range of the meaning of *teaching*, but moves slightly out of the central focus. The *trainer* is a teacher, but not quite a model of the *teacher*. When we are training, we are engaged in teaching, but all teaching is not training. The concepts are related, but not identical. One concept cannot be directly substituted for the other.

This can be seen by comparing the trainer of animals with the trainer of swimmers. The trainer of animals does not, of course, give reason to his subjects. The trainer of swimmers very likely does. A human subject may improve his performance in a skill if he understands relevant instructions. In this sense, the trainer of animals is further away from the central meaning of *teaching* than the trainer of human beings. This distinction shows up in an expression often used by teachers of the mentally handicapped: "Trainable but not educable." As Green says, "Training resembles teaching insofar as it is aimed at actions which display intelligence."[8] To quote him more fully: "In proportion as training is aimed at a greater and greater display of intelligence, it more and more clearly resembles teaching, and one of the clues as to how closely training approaches teaching is the degree to which it involves explanations, reasons, argument, and weighing evidence. It is because training sometimes approaches this point, that we can in many cases substitute the word 'teaching' for the word 'training' without any change in meaning."[9]

CONDITIONING

Conditioning lies on the border line between teaching and non-teaching. The classical example of conditioning is, of course, Pavlov's dogs learning to salivate when the bell rings. Like training, conditioning aims at changing behavior. But can it count as a species of *teaching?* The following considerations will help decide the matter. We say that Pavlov "conditioned" his dogs to salivate. It would be odd to say that he "trained" them to do so. Even in animal training, there seems to be a presumption that the animal

---

[8] Green, "A Topology of the Teaching Concept," in Macmillan and Nelson (eds.), *Concepts of Teaching: Philosophical Essays*, p. 31.
[9] *Ibid.*

cooperates with some degree of intelligence. We speak, in fact, of an animal than can learn complicated tricks as an "intelligent" animal. Surely, no one would say this of Pavlov's dogs. No intelligence of even the most subhuman variety is required for this type of behavioral change, even when it takes place in a human being.

It is possible, for example, to condition a person's pupilary reflex to respond to verbal commands, such as "contract." Even the subject himself may eventually give the command to contract his own pupils, but no intelligence is involved. The subject has no conscious control over his pupilary reactions and cannot improve the situation by trying harder or in some more skilled way. The pupillary reaction is induced in exactly the same way that salivation was induced in Pavlov's dogs.

No doubt, in most training, even in complex behavior like speech, there is an element of conditioning or reinforcement. The concept of *practice* involves some such elements. Though, in the later case, there is a norm observing activity on the part of the learner that transcends the purely reflex activity of the body. As the practicer advances in his skill he discriminates wrong from right modes of *practicing*. A pianist, for instance, will repeat certain passages in order to imprint, so to speak, the muscular reactions that are needed to perform the passages correctly. Hence, when the time for performance arrives, he need not think about this part of his playing. It has become automatic.

We will return to this psychological topic at several points in the remaining chapters. It is an important current topic in education. There is a great deal of uncritical acceptance by educators of techniques offered by psychologists who operate within the context of conditioning theories. Their suitability for teachers should be examined carefully.

If *conditioning* lies at the border of permissible meanings of *teach*, it would seem that mere physical threat and intimidation lie outside the pale. Torture, for instance, would undoubtedly, change human behavior, but it could hardly qualify as a species of teaching. Suppose, as William James speculated, your optic nerve were successfully grafted into the auditory centers of the brain so that you could "see" sounds. Would it be correct to say that you had been *taught* to see sounds or that you had *learned* to see them? Surgery, then, belongs outside of both *teaching* and *learning*.

KNOWING AND BELIEVING

The teaching continuum diagram is divided between those activities intended to change behavior (on the left), and those intended to bring about a grasp of some new knowledge or some change in beliefs (on the right). How shall we view this division? Instructing or indoctrinating are concerned with such matters as *true* and *false*, correct and faulty *reasoning, evidence,* and so on. Training and conditioning, on the other hand, do not involve such questions. There is no problem of *truth* in inducing pupilary contraction; the issue is one of success or failure.

If we come to *know* or to *believe* something, we suppose it to be *true.* There are many ways in which we may be said to *know* or to *believe* something, and these are relevant to teaching, especially when we wish to distinguish, say, the kind of believing that results from *indoctrination,* and that which is aimed at *instructing,* or in the most fundamental sense of *teaching.*

The logic of belief systems is, therefore, highly relevant to certain elements in the concept of teaching. Green points out the contrast between "holding beliefs evidentially and non-evidentially."[10] A belief held evidentially is one that is subject to change through rational criticism. Many beliefs are not of this character. Some beliefs, such as those held by virtue of their function within the psychology of the individual, are not held evidentially. Beliefs of this sort form a psychological system, but not necessarily a logical system. Within the psychological system, some beliefs are more fundamental than others, but they are functionally central rather than logically primitive. If attacked, they will no doubt be defended by so-called *reasons,* but these will, upon inspection, prove to be rationalization. Moreover, when the alleged *reasons* for a psychologically central belief are refuted, the belief is not abandoned; the be-

[10] *Ibid.,* p. 43.

liever simply retrenches with fresh rationalizations. Even contradictions among such beliefs may not move the believer because he has developed mechanisms for keeping these clusters of beliefs isolated from others. Thus, a firm believer in *democracy* may also remain racially prejudiced despite the inconsistencies which may appear among the elements in his belief. The inconsistencies are themselves masked by rationalization or protected by the simple device of not thinking of the two incompatible items at the same time.

These observations have an important bearing on the meaning of *teaching*. The intention of teaching is rationally or evidentially held beliefs. The person instructing, for instance, is subject to questions concerning the reasonable grounds of the beliefs he is seeking to convey.

This raises several questions. One is the status of *indoctrination* as a mode of teaching. Another is the relationship between knowing and doing, or understanding and performing. Let us consider the latter issue first. To do this, we will have to examine several related concepts, such as *telling* and *drilling*.

UNDERSTANDING AND PERFORMING
TELLING AND DRILLING

Komisar argues for a distinction between the teacher intending that the student *understand* something and intending that he *learn* something. Imagine, he suggests, that we "go through the proof of some theorem (T) in such a way as to get an auditor to recognize it *as* proof of T."[11] To accomplish that, he writes, "we would not so much expose the reasoning . . . as drill the students in the steps seriatim."[12] I doubt that he can make this distinction stick.

Would we say that the student had *learned* the theorem if he could parrot the proof without understanding? He would certainly have learned something, namely to parrot certain words. Would

[11] Paul B. Komisar, "Teaching: Act and Enterprise," in Macmillan and Nelson (eds.), *Concepts of Teaching: Philosophical Essays*, p. 76.
[12] *Ibid.*, p. 77.

that count as having learned the theorem? Or, conversely, would we say that he had not learned anything about the proof if he understood but could not repeat it? No doubt, the student who could repeat the proof with understanding would have learned in a more significant sense than in either of the other cases. In this case, the teacher would have succeeded in his intention more fully. There is a meaning of *learning* in the sense of rote repetition as well as in the sense of *coming to understand*. *Coming to understand* coupled with the capacity to express that understanding in relevant ways more adequately states the intention of the act of teaching than either of these elements.

It may clarify the distinctions we are making to note another teaching word, *telling*. "I told him about X" is not quite the same as "I instructed him in X." "I demonstrated X to him" lies somewhere between the two concepts. Telling is certainly a part of teaching, but it is not enough. Telling a pupil that $6 \times 7 = 42$ is not really *teaching* him that this is so. It is only when the teacher aims at the pupil's understanding, why is the product of 6×7, that he can be said to have been *taught* this subject matter. Komisar would say that the student had not *learned* unless he could somehow do the sum himself after forgetting the way in which it was explained, even if he had really understood the explanation of it at the time. Certainly, being able to do the sum one's self is a reasonable addition to mere understanding, but it does not preclude saying that understanding alone is a kind of learning in its own right. To say that *drill* would have been used if learning had been the goal is to fail to see that *drill* without understanding is as defective, if not more defective, as a teaching procedure than rational demonstration without drill. The drilled student would, no doubt, be able to perform the drilled behavior, but he would not know what he was doing and would not, therefore, be able to perform similar assignments because he would not see the formal likenesses. On the other hand, the student who once understood would, in most cases, be able to recover that understanding and practice to become skilled, not only in this particular problem, but in others of the same order.

Referring again to the continuum of the teaching chart, we

should notice that *drilling* belongs with instructing as a mean of inculcating knowledge or changing beliefs. Yet it has strong affinities to training and conditioning on the side of the chart dealing with changes in behavior. *Drill* can be properly viewed as a kind of training (or *practicing*) that aims at an ability to perform verbally. There is no question of its required use by the educator. It is especially appropriate in the audio-lingual method of teaching languages, in memorizing basic information like the multiplication table, and so on. Here understanding is at a minimum or may even be virtually absent. In saturation language courses of the audio-lingual variety, any reference to dictionaries, written symbols, grammar, or the logical structures of languages is held to have a negative influence on the rate of learning. What is demanded is the instantaneous imitated response in the new language—even when the speaker does not have the slightest notion of what he is saying.

Drill is of the essence in such instruction, and no one would deny that instructors in such sessions were teaching. Their pupils often become proficient in a very short time. The drill, however, would fail in its purpose if the pupils remained in the parrot stage of the course. Gradually, as the verbal responses become habitual, the student finds himself *thinking* in the new language. He associates meanings and understands concepts as in his native tongue. A person who could merely rattle off correct responses to stock questions in French exercises would not have learned French unless he came to understand the meaning of the stock questions and answers. The instructor awaits the time when his student can converse about matters that have not been presented for drill. The test of his mastery comes in this wider context where lack of understanding would reveal a fatal deficiency. The reason that the original stock phrases become pregnant with meaning is that they are used over and over again in relevant contexts. The student is doing more than drilling. He is observing situations in which the words are appropriate and responding to them intelligently.

Thus, there is a lattice of logical connections among such concepts as *telling, instructing, demonstrating, explaining,* and *drilling* as forms of teaching aimed at, but not requiring, *learning.* Not "requiring," because, as we have seen, *teach* is a *task* word, not an achievement word.

INDOCTRINATING

Thus far we have seen that a number of concepts like telling, instructing, demonstrating, and drilling belong to that side of the teaching continuum concerned with inculcating new knowledge or changing beliefs. What is the status of *indoctrinating*? Is it teaching? Our answer is that it belongs to the teaching continuum, but only at its edge, and, as in the case of *conditioning*, with reservations. This shows again how fuzzy some of the boundaries are among the various parts of the territory we call *teaching*. Indoctrination can be viewed as a form of *telling*, accompanied by a special rationale. Green puts it well when he says that "the intent of indoctrination is to lead people to hold beliefs as though they were arrived at by inquiry, and yet to hold them independently of any subsequent inquiry and therefore secure against the threat of change by the later introduction of conflicting reasons or conflicting evidence."[13] The views held as a result of indoctrination are thus held nonevidentially.

The paradigm of *indoctrination* that naturally comes to mind is a priest teaching the catechism. In its narrowest sense, this may be mere *telling* and *drilling* to assure that the pupil can recite the proper answers to the catechetical questions whether he understands them or not. This is, no doubt, a caricature of catechism classes. In actual practice, the meaning of the catechism is usually more or less explained, and, depending upon the sophistication of the priest, reasons are offered on behalf of the standard answers. If one were to hear the instruction, he might even consider it an instance of teaching in the paradigmatic sense of attempting to bring about an understanding of evidential beliefs.

White in his essay on indoctrination identifies the factor that distinguishes what is going on here from teaching in the paradigmatic sense, namely, that the priest aims at "fixing the pupil's beliefs so that they are unshakable."[14]

It is well to sort out the essential nature of indoctrination from

[13] Green, "A Topology of the Teaching Concept," in Macmillan and Nelson (eds.), *Concept of Teaching: Philosophical Essays*, p. 44.

[14] J. P. White, "Indoctrination," in R. S. Peters (ed.), *The Concept of Education*, p. 182.

its theological context for two reasons. First, in modern education, scarcely anyone supposes that it is the task of public school teachers to teach religious doctrines in this way. The modern concern over indoctrination is, therefore, over something broader than the subject matter of religious doctrines. The second reason is that almost any subject matter can be the content of indoctrination. Child-centered theorists of education, for instance, regard all traditional methods of teaching as indoctrination. Indoctrination is then any method of instruction that aims at "fixing the pupil's beliefs so that they are unshakable."[15] This could apply as well to a nontheological subject, such as patriotism or morality.

Are teaching and indoctrination compatible? If teaching must carry with it a rationale that is capable of being understood by the pupil, then indoctrination would seem to lie outside the pale of teaching. Some will complain that indoctrinators very often give reasons for their views. No doubt, but we have seen that there is a difference. The reasons that are given in teaching are always, in a theoretical sense, contradictable. Teaching implies an unfinished inquiry into the logic or meaning of a subject matter, and the unfinished nature of the inquiry means that the beliefs are at no stage strictly "unshakable." In principle, they are subject to expansion, revision, or even contradiction. Of course, it would be absurd to suppose that one might change his fundamental principles every other day. Some beliefs exhibit a quasi-permanent status. The difference in principle is nonetheless important, and a student who would *come to understand* must realize the tentative and challengeable character of all his learning if he is to escape being the subject of indoctrination.

I suspect that merely knowing that one was being indoctrinated would set a limit to its success. If one were to say to a student, "I am now going to indoctrinate you," he would be in a good position to question the whole scheme, and, no doubt, would do so. Similarly, the person who said, "I hold the views to which I have been indoctrinated to be true," would already imply that he had other reasons for holding them. If he did not have some additional reasons, he would be like the person who says, "I hold these

[15] *Ibid.*

proven views to be unproven." Or, "I hold these false views to be true." Or, "I hold these uncertain and doubtful views to be unquestionable." All these sound odd because they *are* odd.

It may be well and good to say that teaching logically excludes indoctrination, but the story is more complicated. White confesses that he first faced up to this question when he considered how much of his own field of political science appeared to be vulnerable to the accusation of indoctrination. It is relatively easy to avoid indoctrination in areas where rational accounts of subject matter are available, and where public verification leads to a consensus of informed investigators. However, in the realms of religion, political beliefs, and morals, where deep differences exist between men of equal intelligence and goodwill, the problem is complex.

White believes that in these realms indoctrination is inevitable. Teachers, he thinks, will inevitably indoctrinate where they cannot determine an issue with reason. Hare, for instance, believes that moral judgments cannot be rationally justified since they are based upon what he calls "decisions of principle."[16] It would then seem that morality would have to be indoctrinated or left out of the educational enterprise. Since, as we shall see, education itself is based upon moral assumption—doing something good for people— a flaw is thereby introduced into the very foundation of education itself. Is there a way out of this difficulty?

Without disputing Hare's characterization of morals at this point, let us expand his principle. There is a contingent or decisional element in all human knowledge in the sense that it rests upon ultimate assumptions that are not themselves rationally provable. Science, for instance, could not proceed without the assumption of some order in nature that is within our comprehension if we investigate further. This assumption of comprehensible order is a kind of scientific *faith* if you will, but *unproven* does not mean arbitrary or whimsical. It is hard to imagine human existence without some such assumption. Its denial would subvert not only science but common sense as well. Democracy is also based upon unprovable assumptions about the powers of men to govern them-

[16] For Hare's ethical theory see his *The Language of Morals* (New York: Oxford University Press, 1952), and *Freedom and Reason* (New York: Oxford University Press, 1963).

selves, and the foolishness of allowing any single group of men to have unlimited power over their fellows. This kind of assumption is not provable, but it is vindicated in experience. The same argument would be used by a Christian, Jew, or Buddhist who has also made a decision of principle about his style of life.

The point is that since human knowledge has this contingent and decisional character, there is no escape from indoctrination by eliminating every scrap of subject matter from education that cannot be grounded empirically in the consensus of inquirers. The solution to our problem would rather seem to lie in another direction, namely, to teach students the contingent character of human knowledge and evaluation as soon as they are able to grasp such a concept. Faiths, whether political, religious, social, or moral, will find their place in the educational process, but students must be initiated into an understanding of the grounds upon which these are so diversely held.

No doubt, this requires a rare kind of detachment on the part of an educator, rare, but not impossible. No doubt, the believer in democracy will tend to indoctrinate rather than to teach, but a full-fledged teaching enterprise will include the detachment that leads students into a full understanding of the kind of human commitment a democratic faith really is.

According to this view, indoctrination belongs to the sphere of teaching even if on the margins and with fuzzy lines of demarcation between legitimate and illegitimate forms of indoctrination.

ENABLING BELIEFS

Green makes another proposal that suggests the same outcome. He points out that among the class of nonevidential beliefs there is a subclass that can be rationally justified in a nonevidential way. He calls these "enabling beliefs." An example of such an enabling belief is a conviction of the value of truth. The value of truth cannot be empirically proven, partly because any empirical argument on its behalf would have to assume its truth. Is the teacher who instructs his pupils in the value of truth indoctrinating? Yes. He wants his pupils to have an unshakable conviction on the subject. Is he justified in this? Yes, says Green, because this belief is not a belief in any particular truth, but a belief that enables men to come to any truth at all. "A deep conviction concerning the value of truth," he writes, "is in this sense rationally defensible because without it there can be no rational defense of any belief whatsoever."[17] Green's further comments on this point:

> It is not, therefore, the aim of teaching to eliminate all passionate convictions. The aim, on the contrary, is to seek every possible assurance that our passionate convictions, our enabling beliefs, are also rationally or evidentially held. Such enabling beliefs may be open for examination, capable of refinement and elaboration, but under no conditions can they be exchanged for others. Their abandonment cannot be warranted on the basis of evidence or reasons, because they are precisely those beliefs without which we could not seriously entertain the evidence.[18]

I think that the words "evidentially held" are a slip of the pen. It is well to keep the notion of "evidential belief" for those beliefs that require empirical evidence. I would say that enabling beliefs are "rationally held," but not "evidentially held."

Are there other beliefs that qualify in this way? None, I suspect that fit the Cartesian turn so neatly as belief in the value of truth. There are other candidates, such as belief in goodwill, or justice, and probably belief in some order of better or worse among values. The denial of any of these would preclude most of the inquiries and decisions that are essential not only to education, but to any form of civilized human existence.

Indoctrination, thus hedged with these several qualifications, would seem to belong legitimately to the teaching continuum.

At this stage, the major outlines of the territory we call *teaching* should be coming into focus. More details will be added as we turn to a related subject, the concept of *learning*.

---

[17] Green, "A Topology of the Teaching Concept," Macmillan and Nelson (eds.), *Concepts of Teaching: Philosophical Essays*, p. 53.
[18] *Ibid.*

5

LEARNING

Analyzing the concept of *learning* poses difficulties that did not appear in the study of the *teaching* concept. There is no paradigm of *learning* as there was for *teaching*, and therefore no comparable way of logically relating various kinds of learning to one another as we did in our treatment of teaching. This makes the definition of learning—the discovery of the *necessary* and *sufficient* criteria for something to count as *learning*—more difficult.

This is not to say that we do not know how to use the word in ordinary language. In ordinary usage, the strands of meaning that make up the cord we call "learning" are more frayed than in the case of teaching.

It is widely presumed that the concept of *learning* has attained clarity among psychologists. Let us begin with this claim. In challenging it, we will discover that we will also be examining another claim, namely, that psychologists possess, or are about to possess, the key to the business of learning.

THE PSYCHOLOGICAL DEFINITION OF LEARNING

Psychologists say a great deal about the "psychology of learning." On the face of it, this would suggest that educators would do well to turn to them for empirically grounded suggestions both for a definition of learning and how to do their job. There are good reasons for bringing both of these views into question. Consider first the problem of definition.

According to most psychologists, *learning* is the relatively permanent modification of behavior as the result of experience. Experiments in learning generally deal with the methods by which such behavioral modifications may be brought about. Is all learning of this sort? I think not. In the first place, learning may take place without the modification of behavior. In some cases, the modification of behavior is at most a probable evidence that learning has taken place. Consider an example in the previous chapter. An instructor goes through a proof in geometry so that the student understands that proof. Suppose that a few minutes later the student cannot duplicate the proof. Would we say that he had not learned *anything*? Or suppose that he could duplicate the proof, but never bothered to do so. Would we say he had learned nothing? All we could say was that we had no behavioral evidence that he had learned something.

On the other hand, suppose that he did duplicate the proof. Would that be evidence that he had *learned the proof* in the fundamental sense of having "understood" it? Not at all. He may have a facile memory so that he can duplicate the proof without understanding. In this case, his behavior cannot stand as the sole meaning of his learning. To repeat: He might behave in the required way without having learned in the most significant sense of the instructor's intention (namely to "understand" the proof), and he might not be inclined to (or be able to) duplicate the proof, and still have learned something significant.

The significance of this example becomes more apparent if we expand it to ask, "What is the behavioral equivalent of understanding mathematics?" Doing mathematical operations? Yes, but specifically which mathematical operations? All of them? That is absurd. Just those that one understands (has learned)? How could we reasonably exhaust the class of understood mathematical operations for any given person? Typical operations, then? How do we know we have touched on every kind of mathematical operation the person has learned? Suppose we have a mathematical genius. He may perform operations no one has ever performed. The point should be clear: There is no behavioral *equivalent* for the state of having come to *understand mathematics*. The best we could hope for would be some kind of behavior as *evidence* of understanding.

The linguistic theorist Naom Chomsky points out that when a child has *learned a language* at even the most elementary level, the number of possible meaningful sentences that he could understand in that language is of orders of magnitude greater than the number of seconds remaining in his life.[1] The *behavioral equivalent* of having *learned a language* is then empirically impossible to arrange even in principle.

The relationship of learning to behavior, then, turns out to be equivocal. This becomes even clearer when we note that behavior may change significantly without any learning. A person's behavior may alter significantly simply because he *decides* to do something he already knows how to do. Suppose, suggests one critic, a bank cashier *decides* to become an embezzler. His behavior will change significantly, but not due to learning. Or, again, suppose a person accidentally sprains his ankle. This is certainly *an experience*, and his behavior changes from walking to limping, but he has not *learned* this new behavior. The formula "either inherited or learned" would seem to be inadequate in the light of such instances.

Since this is an important issue in educational theory, let us

---

[1] Naom, Chomsky, *Language and Mind* (New York: Harcourt Brace Jovanovich Inc., 1968), p. 10.

consider the psychological point of view further. Hardie claims that all learning is one of two types. Type one is a case of learning to give old responses to new stimuli. The classical instance is Pavlov's dogs learning to salivate at the sound of a bell. Type two is the reinforcement of a selected item of behavior by rewarding that behavior every time it occurs so that, in the future, it will occur with a high degree of regularity. An example of this later type is the hungry pigeon that pecks at random until it accidentally touches a button that releases food. The reward leads again to the desired behavior which is again rewarded. As the number of reinforcements increases undesired responses become fewer and the desired response becomes fixed. The pigeon has *learned* to peck the button when it is hungry. Thus, Hardie says, "learning is the building, more or less permanently, of new associations; and the associations must be either between a response (already tied to one stimulus) and a new stimulus or between a response (untied), and a stimulus that had not been associated together before."[2] Hardie commends this account because, as he says, "A description of both types of learning can be given without any reference to internal, unobservable, mental processes."[3]

In Hardie's arguments it is not hard to detect opinions strongly reminiscent of the empiricist criterion of meaning that reigned during the logical-empiricist phase of the history of analysis. (See Chapter 1.) This is what Peters calls the Hobbes-Hull-Skinner thesis. Hull is the celebrated psychologist who systematically formulated the theory of learning embodied in Hardie's type one. Skinner is famous for his formulation of type two, the reinforcement theory of learning. The seventeenth-century philosopher Hobbes is the most celebrated modern exponent of materialism. He contended for a world view in which everything is merely matter in motion.

Peters' characterization thus places this learning theory as a species of materialist metaphysics, a reversion to a mode of thought rejected by analysts. I suggested earlier that analytic thinkers, be-

[2] C. D. Hardie, "Two Commentaries on Learning," in B. Paul Komisar and C. J. B. Macmillan, *Psychological Concepts in Education* (Skokie, Ill.: Rand McNally, 1967), p. 153.
[3] *Ibid.*

longing as they do to the empirical tradition, sometimes show a softness toward materialism from time to time despite their low estimate of metaphysical theories. Peters' objections to this learning theory are analytical. Of course, no thinking can go on if the nervous system is not in order, but this in no sense means that we can learn about thought from inspecting the body. Peters comments as follows: ". . . We cannot begin to describe what we mean by performances such as remembering, perceiving, and knowing in such terms. For how can we get notions like being right about the past or having good evidence for what we say by studying the movements of the body or brain? We have to understand human conventions and human language and the criteria in terms of which actions and statements are assessed."[4]

Peters distinguishes between *happenings* and *actions*. *Happenings*, such as an eye blink, occur, but actions, such as winking, are something we do. Learning the former is not the same as learning to perform the latter. As he says, "human goings-on are not all of a piece" and there "cannot therefore be any one type of explanation for them, any one type of learning."[5]

Another difficulty with the behaviorist's theory of learning lies in the ambiguity of the notion of a *stimulus*. To say that a person blinks his eye due to the stimulus of a puff of air against the eyeball is clear enough, but what is the *stimulus* for a wink?[6] A wink is a social act set in a situation that cannot be explained by reference to mere physical stimuli. Events that evoke a wink must have a meaning. This meaning is inseparable from the way a person views the world in which he lives. You cannot understand the wink until you understand the actor's understandings, valuings, and perceptions. Also, you cannot do this without entering a symbolic realm that has no strict behavioral (physical) or observable counterpart.

Green clarifies this distinction between a *happening* and an *action*. Where happenings are under consideration, we can be said to have acquired a disposition to act "in *conformity* to rule,"

[4] R. A. Peters, *Authority, Responsibility, and Education* (New York: Atherton Press, 1966), p. 124.
[5] *Ibid.*, p. 125.
[6] *Ibid.*

whereas in the case of *actions*, we have acquired a disposition to act "in *obedience* to rule."[7] A rat that has learned to run a maze correctly can be said to have acquired a disposition to behave "in conformity to rule." There is, after all, a correct way to run the maze, but the rat could not be said to have behaved in this manner by having *considered* the rule. "To learn to obey a rule," writes Green, "is not simply to acquire a disposition to act in a certain way, but a disposition to act in that way *because* it is a correct way."[8] Since a great deal of human learning is of this sort, it is false that all learning falls within the categories of conditioned-operant learning as claimed by Hardie and many psychologists. Furthermore, it follows from this inadequacy of behaviorist psychology that while some human behavior may be *explained* by discovering likely *causes*, other human activity can only be understood by finding *reasons*.

One possible objection to this distinction comes from psychologists of the Freudian persuasion. If we accept the apparently reasonable proposition that all behavior is motivated, we open the door to the psychologist who deals in subconscious or unconscious motivation. His claim is that all so-called *rational* behavior is essentially nonrationally motivated, and that the alleged *reasons* for the activity are merely rationalizations. The agent, then, is really not an agent at all, he is the pawn of unconscious forces. I am not sure how the Freudian and Skinnerian psychologists get their respective theories to form a consistent system, but together they would seem to give a fairly good argument against what I have been calling rational activity. Can anything decisive be said against this argument? I think it can.

Suppose A gives what he thinks to be a genuine *reason* (as distinct from a causal *explanation*) for some activity. B remarks that he knows why A holds this view, namely, for nonrational psychological causes unknown to A. C comes along and points out that B holds this view not because of the *reasons* he sets forth, but because of nonrational psychological causes in his own psyche. D comes along,

[7] Thomas Green, "Teaching, Acting, and Behaving," in Komisar and Macmillan (eds.), *Psychological Concepts in Education*, p. 195.
[8] *Ibid*.

and so forth. Surely, if there is anything at all to the notion that sometimes men hold their views for nonrational *causes* other than their public announced *reasons*, this can be maintained only if some other men (psychologists, perhaps) hold their views of such behavior for genuine reasons. If no one has rational grounds for his opinions, then no one can validly assert as *true* that anyone else is holding his views for nonrational causes. If anyone can have rational opinions, then others, beside psychologists, may also hold them. In short, the universalization of the doctrine of nonrationality is self-contradictory.

A more linguistic argument can be given for this same position. The notion of *rationalization* presupposes the notion of *rational*. A rationalization is a pseudoreason that has only the form of reason. No one could rationalize unless he understood to some degree what it was to reason, for in rationalizing, we all want to appear reasonable. This desire to *appear* if not to *be* reasonable makes sense only if there is some meaning to being rational.

Furthermore, if we are to take ordinary language as the standard for our reflection, we cannot relegate the multitude of discussions about reasons (in science, morality, or practical affairs) to the limbo of nonsense. This distinction clearly exists in ordinary talk, and it is not the product of some philosophical theory, it is simply there. To reject it is to opt for a revisionist metaphysic of the Hobbesian variety. It is hard to see how this view could be the considered product of analytic reasoning. Consider, finally, the anomaly of the philosopher who reasons that all reasons are rationalizations.

This discussion of psychology illustrates how many facets there are to the simple question of finding out what we mean by *learning*. The upshot of our inquiry thus far is that the behavioristic approach is inadequate. Behavior, it turns out, is neither *sufficient* nor *necessary* for something to count as *learning*. This does not mean that the *psychology of learning* is not about learning. No one could question this. Rats indeed *learn* to run mazes. This is not, as Hardie seems to suggest, a paradigm of *learning* the way Socrates instructing Meno's slave is a paradigm of *teaching*.

Lacking such a paradigm, we may not be able to state clearly what *learning* is, but we can still look at linguistic usage to make some interesting and useful distinctions.

OTHER APPROACHES TO
THE DEFINITION OF "LEARNING"

One proposal to facilitate the making of useful distinctions in the learning concept is to sort out learning by the thing learned. The trick is to substitute "learning X" for "learning." Thus, the proposal goes, learning to run a maze is a different kind of learning than learning a language. This lead is valuable because we certainly must note important differences among such things as learning to run mazes, learning to speak a language, learning to value something, learning that something is true, learning to believe in something, and so on. It is doubtful that this helps us with the concept of learning as such. Learning X, whatever X may be, is always simply a case of learning. None of these *learnings* turns out to be more or less central to learning than any others. Simply considering them as *learning* does not cut the *learning* pie in a logical way. Most of these distinctions, as Green has argued, turn out to be distinctions in teaching. Thus indoctrination (a method of teaching) may be a way of bringing about someone's learning (for example) that "X is true when X is false." This illuminates more clearly what we mean by such learning than when the reference to the teaching process is omitted.

A more promising suggestion is to direct our attention not to the subject matter learned, but to the *mode* of learning. In the section that follows, we will examine several important modes. However, again, I find myself in agreement with Green: these distinctions turn out to be differences that stem from the logic of the teaching concept rather than from the learning concept. The reasons for this will become more apparent as these various modes of learning are examined. Before leaving our present topic, however, let us note briefly some educational applications of our analysis to this point.

SOME CONCLUSIONS ABOUT
THE PSYCHOLOGY OF
LEARNING AND EDUCATION

The first conclusion from this analysis is that psychological studies of learning may not necessarily be of interest to teachers. The psychologist may discover all sorts of ways to induce learning that could not count as *teaching*. Jestingly, I once suggested to a student that she could learn something the way the rats learn to run mazes. Her reply was, "I don't want to get that hungry." Very hungry rats learn to run mazes more quickly than well-fed ones. Would keeping students very hungry and rewarding them with bits of food as they responded in desired ways count as a teaching method?

Or, more drastically, perhaps rats learn to run mazes more efficiently when they are subjected to electric shocks at appropriate times. Would we say that wiring students' desks counted as a teaching method? The psychologist might reply that our reluctance to use such methods is due simply to our present moral values. If we were less squeamish, we might become better teachers. Green points out that a change in our ethics would not change the logic of the teaching concept.[9] The distinctions that were made between *indoctrination* and *instruction* or between *conditioning* and *training* would hold regardless of a teacher's ethics. The notion of *teaching* is ethically neutral, and our analysis of these distinctions is a logical, not an ethical matter.

This doubt about the applicability of psychology to education goes against the grain of most publications on the psychology of learning. Edward Best, in his essay on "The Suppressed Premise in Educational Psychology," points out that in many such publications a suppressed moral "should" is presupposed. Authors assume without argument that given a successful experiment in psychology, the new procedure should be used by educators. My point is that the logic of the intermediate moral exhortation must be spelled out carefully before we know whether or not the psychological material is useful to teachers.

When, for example, Hull and others discovered that *need reduction* functions in learning situations with rats, some writers immediately suggested that teachers use the *needs* of their students as counters in the teaching game by *reducing* these needs as rewards (and therefore motivation) for learning. I am not arguing that this is bad. What I want to point out is that this proposal poses a host

---

[9] Green, "A Topology of the Teaching Concept," in Macmillan and Nelson (eds.), *Concepts of Teaching: Philosophical Essays*, pp. 60–61.

of educational questions that are not even hinted at by the educational psychologists. Here are some of them: What do we mean by *human needs?* Which *needs* should be *reduced?* How are such human needs as the need for status, friendship, knowledge, and so on, best *reduced* for sound educational purposes?

This should be sufficient to warn the educator who is tempted to believe that his task may be made immediately easier by applying psychological materials directly to educational situations.

MODES OF LEARNING: KNOWING *HOW* AND KNOWING *THAT*

Ryle, in his essay on "Knowing How and Knowing That," says that ". . . when a person is said to understand something in the sense of 'shrewd' or 'silly,' 'prudent' or 'imprudent,' the description imputes to him, not the knowledge, or ignorance, of this or that truth, but the ability, or inability, to do certain sorts of things."[10] "In ordinary life," he says, "as well as in the special business of teaching . . . we are much more concerned with people's competences than with their cognitive repertoires, with the operations than with the truths that they learned."[11] Here Ryle opens a new range of meanings for analyzing the concept of learning. To learn in the sense of understanding certainly means to know some facts. But it means more than that. It means the ability to perform certain kinds of acts in accordance with the norms that define the correct performance of those acts. To understand chess is to play well, not simply to state the rules of the game.

This point is important, but it is possible to overrate it. It is true that a good chess player does not rehearse the rules of chess to himself as he plays, but he may rehearse certain strategies. He could not be said to understand chess as fully as someone who could tell us the rules or spell out his strategies. Nor do I think that we would properly say that a computer that plays a good game of chess "understands chess." I suspect that when we say that the machine has

[10] Gilbert Ryle, *The Concept of Mind* (New York: Barnes & Noble, 1949), p. 27.
[11] *Ibid.*, p. 28.

"learned" to play chess, we are using the word "learned" metaphorically. By the conventions of our language organisms *learn*, but inanimate objects do not. If a nail is bent and then straightened, it will tend to bend at the same place when strain is placed upon it. Would we say that the nail *learned* to bend in that particular way? We *might* say this of a plant that was bent in certain ways by the gardener, but here the word *learned* would seem odd. On the other hand, we would say that a dog *learned* to hold its tail in a certain way if it was held in that position repeatedly. As we go down the scale of intelligence and awareness from human beings to animals to plants to stones, the term *learned* becomes increasingly inappropriate.

At the human level, some modicum of memory seems to be required for something to have been *learned*. We would not say that the nail "remembered" where it was bent. *Remembering* refers to the past in a special way, such as getting things correct. We would not say that I "remembered" something that happened yesterday if that event had not occurred. Nor would simple mechanical repetition count as *remembering* similar past events. For human learning at least, some element of remembering seems to be involved. To perform some activity correctly means more than the ability to repeat it in accordance with a rule for that performance. It means to refer the present performance to the past in such a way that it is done *because* the person recalls that this is the way it should be done. The computer that plays chess does not remember anything. The machine cannot make any reference whatsoever to the past. Its behavior and structure are strictly present tense.

It is true, as Ryle points out, that the intelligent man does not always rehearse the reasons for his proper action. This does not means that his memory is not involved in his performance. In hard cases, he may indeed rehearse his reasons for a given action. Even in this type of case, however, Ryle is correct in pointing out that general reflections never add up to understanding without the test of appropriate action. On this he says, "Knowing how to apply maxims cannot be reduced to, or derived from, the acceptance of (general) . . . maxims."[12]

[12] *Ibid.*, p. 31.

Human learning then includes both knowing *that* and knowing *how*. Yet, it certainly includes more. A child could not be said to understand (to have learned) that one should keep quiet while others are talking if he was in the habit of interrupting. He might, in a factual sense, know *that* it was not proper. He might also know *how* to remain silent by simply stopping. Until he performed what he knew, until he was *disposed* to remain quiet at appropriate times, he could not be said to have really learned.

Ryle makes another point in this connection. "To perform intelligently," he writes, "is to do one thing and not two things. . . ."[13] Nor is it to do three things: "Being quiet while others speak," shows itself in being appropriately quiet, and when this is fully understood the child simply does it at the right time. He does not rehearse mentally some facts or principles, then invoke his *disposition* to act in this way, and then, at last, quiet down. These things are all of one piece. This does not prevent our discovering by analysis that his activity includes all three things. The reasons are clear: The child may indeed be able (1) to rehearse the rule about being quiet (without being quiet), (2) to show that he can be quiet when he wants to (without being quiet at the proper time), and (3) to demonstrate his disposition to behave in this way by being quiet appropriately. Only the full range of these *knowings* is what we mean by the child understanding that he should be quiet while others speak.

It could also be said that he did not understand what he was doing unless he had some grasp of the meaning of respect for other people, and the conditions for intelligible discourse. Being quiet while others speak is a good rule only in certain settings. To be able to discern the proper setting for invoking the disposition to remain silent is part of understanding the rule. If, for instance, he remained silent during a football game because other people were shouting, we should regard this as odd. Also, in some conversations, if he did not occasionally interrupt to show he understood, his silence might well be misunderstood. Good conversation is not a dialogue of set speeches.

The point of this analysis is that knowing *that* and knowing *how* are closely related in human learning. Also, something more is in-

---

[13] *Ibid.*, p. 40.

volved: a disposition to behave in accordance with both knowledge
and the rules of activity.

LEARNING *DISPOSITIONS*

This notion of a *disposition* deserves more attention. Ryle seems
to treat a *disposition* as though it were similar to the property of a
physical object. To say that the child has the disposition to remain
quiet while others are talking, according to Ryle, would be like saying that glass is brittle, that is, it will, under certain conditions, fly
into small fragments. Is this an adequate account? I think not.

Intelligent, honest, cheerful, and *proud* are disposition words.
Ryle is correct in saying that they imply specific behavior under
certain conditions. An *intelligent* person, given a puzzle, will set to
work in such a way as to solve it. So far, *intelligent* would seem to
be like *brittle,* but there are some important differences. To learn
to be intelligent does not mean to learn a set of automatic responses
to set situations, not even to a very large number of set situations.
To be intelligent means to understand a whole range of rules of
reasons that are relevant in complex ways to uncountable numbers
of potential situations. It means to be aware of a standard.

Moreover, it means to value that standard. A person is not intelligent merely because he has the ability to act in reasonable ways.
He must also prize rationality. He must want to act reasonably.
Without such a positive evaluation of reasonable ways of behaving
he will not invoke his ability to be rational. To say that glass has a
disposition to shatter would be to say that somehow it *wants* to
shatter under the appropriate conditions. Learning to be intelligent,
then, is to learn a disposition, and learning a disposition is a complex mixture of knowing *that,* knowing *how,* and valuing in certain
ways. Valuing is the link between capacity and inclination. Valuing
itself deserves more attention, but we must leave this matter until a
later chapter where it can be explored more extensively.

LEARNING *WHY*

Another mode of human understanding is the ability to answer the
question *why.* To know facts, to have appropriate skills, even to

possess a disposition to perform in certain ways is not a complete account of human learning if one cannot answer *why* questions. *Why* is a complex concept. "Why did the pipes freeze?" might be answered by pointing out that the temperature dropped, or that they were not properly insulated. Another answer might be, "I forgot to drain the system." The later explanation refers to human activity, not to physical laws. Questions like "Why do you regard that as the moral thing to do?" Or, "Why did that happen?" Or, "Why does he behave like that?" require different kinds of answers appropriate to the logos of that subject matter. Even the person who behaves irrationally has some method in his madness. The search for this *why* lies at the base of psychotherapy, and it is surprising how often the answer turns out to be more like answering the *why* of rational behavior (giving reasons) than answering the *why* of purely physical events (giving causal explanations).

It is important to underscore the point that there is no one answer to *why*. Failure to realize it is the source of many confusions. "Why do you prefer that painting to this one?" is a question that normally calls for a different kind of answer than the question "Why do you like your steak well done?" The latter question might be answered by pointing out that work in a slaughterhouse had taken away one's taste for rare meat, or that when one was a child this was the kind of food one learned to like. Explanations of this kind are often sought to questions about preferences in art, but they are beside the point. A preference for one painting rather than another is generally not a question of personal history, but of knowledge about art. There is nothing odd about being conditioned to like certain foods, but taste in music is not purely a matter of conditioning. In fact, a person who would understand art often must overcome his early conditioning in order to be open to the work itself, to allow the logos of art to determine his judgments. He must learn the *why* that is appropriate to judgments about art.

OTHER SENSES OF *LEARN*

There are many other modes of learning that deserve analysis. For instance, it is valuable to distinguish the sense of "learning that X is true" from "learning to believe that X is true." As Komisar says, to say "He learned the secrets of the Chancellory" means that he really knew what those secrets were.[14] The notion of *true* is decisive for this kind of learning. On the other hand, to say "He believes that the secrets of the Chancellory are such and such" does not imply that these are indeed the secrets of the Chancellory.

Another kind of learning mentioned by Komisar is "learning to be," as in learning to be a friend. This he correctly calls "learning in the commital sense."[15] There are reasons for questioning the appropriateness of calling the behavior that follows from commitment or decision a result of learning. We may, however, ask an important educational question: Is it possible to teach commitment or decision? In a later chapter, we shall examine a variety of teaching proposals. Among them will be the call to teach human beings how to relate, how to learn, how to be creative, and so on. Whether or not these can be taught will depend in part upon what we mean by such proposals, and whether that meaning is consonant with what we have learned about teaching.

In the last two chapters, we have sampled analyses of two major concepts in the constellation of education: *teaching* and *learning*. It is time that we turned to the concept of *education* itself.

[14] B. Paul Komisar, "More on the Concept of Learning," in Komisar and Macmillan, (eds.), *Philosophical Concepts in Education*, p. 219.
[15] *Ibid.*, p. 222.

6

EDUCATION

When a student says, "My major is education," he is using "education" in a different sense than when a teacher says, "My business is education." "Education" as a major is a field of academic study; teaching is an activity of *educating*. Analytically, it is useful to keep this distinction in mind. One of the current debates over education as a field of study takes the form of asking," "Is education a discipline?" It is a convenient question for illustrating analytic procedures. The other meaning—education as an activity of *educating* —raises even more important issues. Let us begin with the question of education as a discipline.

IS EDUCATION A DISCIPLINE?

What is a discipline? We sometimes talk about such subjects as physics, chemistry, history, and the romance languages as "disciplines." When we ask a university teacher his discipline, we expect to learn in what academic subject he is expert. Teachers in departments or schools of education are sometimes embarrassed by colleagues who question whether education is a legitimate academic field. The historian of education can tell us that this is not a new dispute. Educationists have been working to legitimize their field for well over a half century. They have succeeded in lifting their enterprise out of the ghetto of the *normal school* and giving it the dignity of departmental or school status in most large universities. Yet there is still considerable condescension from many academic areas. One of the ways to legitimize education as a field of study is to show that it qualifies as a *discipline*.[1] Though there are good reasons for thinking that this is not the most promising approach, an examination of the claim will enable us to clear up some conceptual confusions.

The first order of business is to determine what a *discipline* is. Unfortunately, the term does not have a clear meaning. Ordinary usage does not help us very much here, perhaps because *discipline* is a quasi-technical term, and it is hard to find agreed instances of usage. One approach is to take some instances of undoubted *disciplines* and find out why they are so considered.

The clearest cases come from the sciences. Physics, chemistry, and biology, we will agree, are certainly *disciplines*. Why is this so? At first it may seem plausible to suppose they are accorded this title because they each study a unique subject matter. However, Peters points out, this applies to sciences only in their early stages.[2] To which of these sciences in their present stage of theoretical development would we assign, on the basis of subject matter, the

[1] See John Walton and James L. Kuethe (eds.), *The Discipline of Education* (Madison: University of Wisconsin Press, 1963), for an extensive debate on this topic.

[2] R. A. Peters, Comments on John Walton, "A Discipline of Education," in Walton and Kuethe (eds.), *The Discipline of Education*, p. 17.

study of genetic material like the DNA molecule? This study, though conventionally regarded as a problem in microbiology, involves both chemistry and physics. What of organic chemistry? Or, how would we distinguish the various social sciences from one another on the basis of subject matter? They all study human activity.

Peters suggests a better, if not entirely satisfactory, criterion: "Sciences can only be vaguely distinguished from each other by reference to the types of questions they ask and the types of answers which they give and by the types of procedure which they employ in testing such answers."[3] In spite of this vagueness of the intramural lines separating the various sciences, each nonetheless has a kind of inner coherence that emerges when questions of a similar sort begin to receive systematic answers together with typical techniques for further investigation.

Is education a discipline in this sense? The answer is not promising. The study of education is not limited to a single set of similar questions, nor does it have any single systematic scheme for answering them, to say nothing of techniques uniquely typical to all phases of educational inquiry. Typical questions in education refer to many widely different kinds of activities and problems: teaching and learning, administration, curriculum building, public relations, social policy, and a host of others. Answers to these questions can only be researched by consulting many disciplines, such as philosophy, psychology, sociology, anthropology, and economics. In addition, many of them require knowledge gleaned from related professional fields like law and medicine, or from practical areas like politics. The idea that all this could become a single discipline with a common theoretical structure and technique is beyond any reasonable probability.

Perhaps we could save the case by seeing if education is a discipline in the sense in which one of the so-called humanities, say, English literature or philosophy, is a discipline. This is more promising, because, as we shall see, the chief concern of education is not with the behavior of things, but with the activities of human beings.

[3] *Ibid.*

SCIENCES AND HUMANITIES

In order to take this tack, we must first make some logical distinction between the sciences and humanities. Scholars in the humanities have had their own problems justifying their fields of study in a scientific and pragmatic age. Alburey Castell's analysis of behavior can help at this juncture in our argument. He distinguishes the language of two modes of behavior: *activity* and *process*. This distinction is very like that made by Green between an *action* and a *happening*. Castell asks us to consider an astronomer studying the solar system: "Three separate behaviors are evident: first the behavior we shall call 'astronomizing'; second, the behavior of the astronomer's brain and nervous system; third, the behavior of the solar system."[4]

When we look at our normal ways of talking about these three kinds of behavior, we discover that our language for the first is radically different from the other two. Here are some characteristic words we use in talking about astronomizing: fallible, purposive, experimental, tentative, guided by criteria, reasoned, involving decisions, correctable, meaningful, and so on. None of this vocabulary is appropriate to talk about either the movements of heavenly bodies or the elements of the human nervous system. It would be odd to say, for instance, that the moon was "fallible," "tentative," or "meaningful," or that the brain made "decisions," or "reasoned," or entertained "purposes." There would be point in "correcting" an astronomer's reasoning, but it would make no sense to speak of the moon's orbit or neural impulses as "mistaken." We would not hold the moon "responsible," nor say that the brain had made a bad "decision."

Let us call the language suitable to the behavior of astronomizing "activity" language, and that appropriate to the brain or heavenly bodies "process" language. The difference in the language of the

---

[4] Alburey Castell, *The Self in Philosophy* (New York: Macmillan, 1965), p. 21. Castell's *Philosophy and the Teacher's World* (Eugene: Bureau of Educational Research, School of Education, University of Oregon, 1967) is a fine study of some of the themes of this chapter, especially the distinction between the sciences and the humanities.

two fields is clearly a matter of ordinary usage. This is the way we talk about processes or activities.

It should be obvious that "process" language refers to the topics we study in the sciences. We do not "blame" chemicals for exploding, we blame the man who mixes them. We do not search for the "cause" of a theory, but for the "reasons" underlying it.

This distinction can help in our search for the meaning of the concept of *discipline* in the humanities. The humanities are concerned chiefly with our knowledge of human *activity*, the sciences are concerned with all *processes* whether they occur in or out of the human body. In fact, we rarely use the word *discipline* for the sciences. We simply refer to them as "sciences." *Discipline* is more or less reserved for studies in the humanities.

This distinction may help us in our search for the possible meaning of education as a discipline. If any case at all can be made for using this term for education as a field of study, it would appear to be in the sense of education as a study of human *activity* rather than a study of *processes*. In other words, we might agree that education is not a *science*, and still hold that it is a discipline in the sense as philosophy or literature.

Our language is not as neat as we might wish. Ambiguities arise where the border lines are not clearly established. There is often spirited debate in the universities over whether to classify history with the social sciences or with the humanities. These fuzzy boundaries appear notably wherever we study human behavior by using categories drawn from the physical sciences. We have just sampled that debate in asking whether *conditioning* is a form of teaching or not. *Conditioning* belongs to *process* language rather than to *activity* language; it is concerned with the behavior of the nervous system rather than with meanings.

The almost universal substitution of the term *behavioral sciences* for *social sciences* shows the trend in that field toward fixing these studies as proper sciences. Are sociology and psychology *sciences* in the sense that they are limited to the study of processes? Can they do their work without any reference to the language of *activity*? Substantial arguments rage over this question, especially in psychology. In a celebrated debate between B. F. Skinner and Carl Rogers, Skinner held that psychotherapy is a process phenomenon, while Rogers insisted in talking about it in activity language. Skinner wanted to recondition the patient; Rogers wanted to help him freely reshape his style of life.[5]

The mixture of points of view will no doubt persist in all attempts to explain human behavior, the one place where activity and process intersect. Man is from one point of view an agent, and from another, the product of impersonal forces. It was this fact that long ago gave rise to the debate over free will and determinism, a debate that up to the present would appear to be a draw.

What bearing has this on the question of whether education is a discipline? The decision would seem to depend upon whether the major concerns of education are process topics or activity topics. On this score, I suspect that though education draws some of its material from the sciences, its main reliance is on our warranted knowledge of activities.

O'Connor, for instance, writes: "Ultimately, all the questions that can be asked about a given educational system can be reduced to two: (i) What is held to be valuable as an end? (ii) What means will effectively realize these ends?"[6] His first question is appropriate only to activities. The second question, as we can see from our study of the *teaching* concept, is a mixture of the two. Unfortunately, O'Connor seems to forget this fact when he criticizes educational theory for not being more strictly scientific. Scheffler draws a line around the word *discipline* in this same narrow way. A *discipline*, he writes, "strives to offer a complete, systematic account of some realm of *things* in the world. It seeks a comprehensive body of true principles describing and explaining the realm it takes as its proper object."[7]

The realm of education, he points out, is an important area of human endeavor. It includes schools, subjects, ideals, and social practices. So far so good. The real issue, he continues, is "whether we can establish reliable principles to explain how and why children

[5] Carl R. Rogers, and B. F. Skinner, "Some Issues Concerning the Control of Human Behavior," *Science*, 124, no. 3231 (Nov. 30, 1956), pp. 1057–1066.

[6] O'Connor, *An Introduction to the Philosophy of Education*, p. 7.

[7] Israel Scheffler, "Is Education a Discipline," in Scheffler (ed.), *Philosophy and Education*, p. 65.

learn, schools develop, curricula change, ideals conflict, perceptions alter, societies differ, and standards of taste and culture are formed."[8] In this quotation, Scheffler refers almost exclusively to the process aspect of education. He does, to be sure, throw in *ideals* which is an activity word. The Australian philosopher of education, James Gribble, in his *Introduction to the Philosophy of Education*, observes that "the list of questions he (Scheffler) offers is composed entirely of empirical questions about how or why children learn, schools develop and so on."[9] He suggests that Scheffler ought to have considered such questions as: "What ought children learn? How have schools developed in the past and how ought they develop in the future? In what direction have curricula changed and what direction ought they to change? What standards of taste and culture do we want to pass on to our children?" and so on.[10]

If we assume that education is chiefly a humanistic rather than a scientific study, then the standard by which we will judge whether education is a body of warrantable knowledge, and perhaps a *discipline* in the humanistic sense, will not depend upon demonstrating its relationship to a supporting body of science. If it is more like poetry, philosophy, or literary criticism, the standards will be different. Of course, insofar as education or any other humanistic discipline refers to processes in a warrantable way, it will need the ancillary support of some science. In the main, however, their task will be of a different kind. Gribble fails to remain consistent on this point when he criticizes literary criticism for its lack of grounding in the empirical sciences. In an age when science has great prestige, it is perhaps inevitable that the humanities will suffer by comparison and the hope will keep rising that somehow they can be made into sciences in due time.

THE HUMANE DISCIPLINES

What characterizes the nonscientific disciplines we call the humanities? The sciences concern themselves with the systematic descrip-

[8] *Ibid.*, p. 76.
[9] Gribble, *Introduction to Philosophy of Education*, p. 184.
[10] *Ibid.*

tion of *processes*, the ways of *things*. The humanities are concerned with the account, as systematic as may be, of the logos of *activities*, the ways of *men*. Processes are such things as earthquakes, eclipses, chemical reactions, neural reactions, and the like. Activities are such things as thinking, discovering, creating, choosing, painting, evaluating, writing, composing, appreciating, and theorizing. They all involve the behavior of human agents who love, judge, sacrifice, reverence, decide, risk, lust, cheat, hate, and kill. Insofar as these are grasped as activities and not as processes, they are the subject matter of the humanities. It should be obvious that a great deal of educational behavior is of this same kind: teaching, instructing, indoctrinating, and conditioning.

The categories appropriate to these activities are not those appropriate to processes. The literary critic, for instance, maps a novel —its plot, setting, characters, mood, and so on—so that the reader can make his way intelligently. He is not doing science, but there are public criteria for his performance that allow his fellow critics to judge the quality of his performance. This is warranted knowledge even if it is not science.

Of course, the sciences and the humanities are not absolutely separate. It is not possible to do science, describe processes, without engaging in activities, such as discovering, deciding, thinking, and so on. Nor is it possible to do humanistic thinking without relying on established scientific knowledge. Yet, we are justified in the distinction because of the difference between the two types of labor and because most fields depend, in the main, on one kind of behavior rather than the other.

The humanities are not then some kind of prescientific thinking that eventually aspires to the status of science. They could, no doubt, benefit from an application to themselves of the rigorous analysis that the sciences have enjoyed. Perhaps, one of the reasons that this has not occurred is modernity's long and uncritical romance with the sciences. The temper of our times has not been suited to the task. One of the benefits of analysis is that by viewing concepts in their contextual variety, we are prevented from forcing every kind of thought into a single mold.

Now to apply this rather long lesson: We have discovered two facts: (1) Humanistic studies qualify as *disciplines*, and (2) education is chiefly concerned with human activities rather than processes. Does this justify regarding education as a discipline? I am afraid not. Education's kinship with the humanities is not close enough. It is still too mixed a bag to fit neatly into this pattern. If we seek a more appropriate title, I would suggest *profession* instead.

In case our conclusion—education does not qualify as a *discipline* —is disappointing, perhaps a remark of Everett Hughes will ease the pain. He expresses astonishment that educators "should want to bring themselves down in the world by asking that their work be recognized as among the disciplines."[11] Disciplines, he points out, are passing things—ways of organizing university curricula— but education is a continuing concern of every society. Education is one of the great practical arts, he writes, like "looking after the sick, keeping order, and distributing justice."[12]

EDUCATION AS A PROFESSION

We speak of law and medicine as *professions*. Neither is a science nor a humane discipline. The doctor's professional training includes many of the sciences, but his business is the application of these sciences to the art of healing. Medicine is an applied field.

Education would seem to fit this pattern much better than either that of science or the humanistic disciplines. It is concerned with the practical art of educating each rising generation. To perform its tasks, it must be knowledgeable of both processes and activities, sciences and humanities. It is not simply a field of *knowledge*, it is the application of this knowledge to a specific complex of practical concerns.

It is not clear when a field of practical concern becomes a *profession*, but it would seem to require several things: (1) The area of application must be of considerable social concern like health, education, legal order, or religion. (2) There must be accessible to its

[11] Everett C. Hughes, "Is Education a Discipline?" in Walton and Kuethe (eds.), *The Discipline of Education*, p. 150.
[12] *Ibid.*, p. 149.

practitioners a significant body of theoretical understanding or knowledge. This knowledge need not consist of a single *discipline*. In fact, the professions draw from both sciences and humane disciplines. (3) It must have evolved some criteria or standards of acceptable performance in the field. Such standards become the basis for public certification. Among these standards are not only those that bear on technical proficiency, but also those which are ethical.

On all these counts, education would seem to qualify as belonging to one of the *professions*. Education is certainly one of the major concerns of civilized existence. The questions with which educators deal have as much bearing on the continuance of civilization as either law or medicine. What can be more important for human beings than their systematic initiation into the realm of civilized meanings? What can contribute more to human dignity than this? Surely health is important, an indispensable condition for life itself. So, for the same reason, is at least a minimal number of material possessions, food, clothing, and so on. None of these enters so closely into the matrix of human well being as the mastery of basic meanings. Without these life is not worth living.

To be sure, education's body of warranted knowledge is not quite as tidy as that of medicine or law, but then it is a younger field of study. And, I suspect, its problems are even more complex. It is a matter of debate whether educators perform more or less poorly than their colleagues in other professions, but there is no doubt that in their search for adequate criteria of certification educators have become more and more concerned about standards of performance.

It could also be debated whether the practitioners of an art are the best teachers and theoreticians of it. "Educator" can mean professor of education in a university or teacher in a secondary school. Of course, the professor of education is in the unique position of practicing his art, while he propounds his theories of that art. Agreeing that education is a profession does not settle the question whether the best organization of the study of education is a separate academic department. The professional historian Bernard Bailyn, who has written extensively in the history of education, questions whether the best histories of education can be written by professional educators. Other noneducationists in the universities would, no doubt, agree with him concerning other facets of educational theory and practice.

This is essentially a practical, not a philosophical question. Perhaps the old adage, what is everyone's business is no one's business, might apply here. Peters points out that though education is not a discipline, many disciplines would benefit from taking educational questions to heart in their own investigations. If the psychologist, for instance, were to take seriously the kind of analysis we have made of *teaching*, and begin to consider the problems of learning from that perspective, he would not only benefit educators, but would add a new dimension to his own theoretical equipment and knowledge. Who will raise these questions if not some group of scholars committed professionally to education? The criticisms of Bailyn and others are worth considering. The problem would seem to be how educational theorists can best avail themselves of the expertise of scholars in those disciplines that impinge on educational thought and practice. The hybrid scholar—educational psychologist/sociologist/economist/philosopher/historian—is one solution, but he runs up against the difficulties of one person becoming competent in two fields. It is not within the competence of analytic philosophy to answer these questions. Its job is more modest: to clarify the formulations of the problem to be solved.

OTHER CHARACTERIZATIONS OF THE EDUCATOR'S ROLE

We have established that the educator may indeed qualify as a "professional," if not as the master of a discipline or science. There are some other role words that are interesting when associated with educating. One of them is the now nearly archaic word "calling." In ecclesiastical circles, the expression "a call to the ministry" or "priesthood" is still in use. With the progressive secularization of society, however, the religious beliefs that made the concept of *calling* meaningful have little hold on the general public. To be sure, the latinized word "vocation" literally means "calling," but it has attained a different meaning.

Job and *vocation* are now almost equivalents. One speaks of having a job as a plumber or having the vocation of plumbing almost interchangeably. Dictionaries of *vocations* list *jobs* by the hundreds. Gone from ordinary language is the meaning that the poet Shelley expressed in his "Hymn of Intellectual Beauty." When overshadowed by an ecstatic experience of beauty, he wrote, "I have vowed that I would dedicate my powers/ To thee and thine—have I not kept the vow?"

Something like a secularized *calling* seems to be involved in teaching and educating. Even the word "profession" once had religious significance, as in "profession of faith." A *professor* once *stood* and *witnessed* for something. I suspect that this is one of the reasons why it seems important to claim professional status, not merely as a mark of competence, but as a mark of the significance of that competence. This connotation is now almost missing in such expressions as "professional musician" or "professional athlete" to designate those who make their living as musicians or athletes, and to distinguish them from the amateur who performs out of "love" for the activity.

This overtone of a secularized *witness* or *calling* clings to the notion of *teacher*, perhaps, because, like health or legitimate and just public order, it is felt to be a great human concern. Thus, teaching is not merely a *career*, much less merely a *job*. It carries the significance of a life-long commitment.

Career is another role word that is interesting. It is closer to *calling* than to *job*. It conveys the notion of a life-consuming devotion to some activity of high value. When we speak of a "stage career," we suggest a fulfillment of some larger range of a person's own talents and abilities rather than the *job* of acting. This expression also suggests some degree of public acclaim, as in speaking of the "career of a surgeon." The question, for instance, may be asked whether a woman can combine a career with marriage. We speak of "interrupting her career" to have children, for example, but not of "interrupting her job." She may "leave" her *job*, but she "interrupts" or even "sacrifices" her *career*.

Reflections of this kind serve to help in the identity of the teacher and educator. If he is to undertake his task with the kind of pointedness and dedication that the work requires, he must have some concept of his work that will permit, even demand, his identification of himself with it. To say, "I am a teacher," or "I am an educator," should be a proud personal profession.

We may now turn to our second meaning of *education*, namely education as the activity of educating.

7

EDUCATING

I am going to argue that "to educate" is to bring about intentionally some kind of understanding, coupled with a disposition to use that understanding in appropriate ways. To educate is an activity engendering essential meanings. To be an educated person means to have acquired an understanding of some considerable range of civilized meanings and a disposition to live by them. If this hypothesis is anywhere near the mark, then *educating* is logically closer to *teaching* than to *learning*. Yet, as we shall see, one's education is not necessarily limited to what he has been taught. Many factors other than teaching may serve to engender essential meanings. Unfortunately, a consideration of nonteaching factors would lead us afield from our major center of interest, namely, the relationship of schools and teaching to the business to educating.

We would not say that a person who had been merely conditioned, or trained, or indoctrinated was *educated*. Teaching, as we have seen, includes all of these in some way or another. We also saw that, in its paradigmatic sense, teaching seeks to awaken the student's understanding and dispose him to behave in ways relevant to that understanding. Teaching, then, aims ultimately at educating.

Teaching "aims" at this goal, but, because it bears a *task* meaning rather than an *achievement* meaning, the teacher may not succeed in his aim. *Educating*, on the other hand, is an *achievement* word. To say "He was educated at Harvard" means that he really was educated. This has a different sense than "He went to Harvard for four years." "He got his education in the school of hard knocks" carries the same achievement sense. He really was educated in this way.

Peters notes another meaning of educating. He maintains that "to educate" carries with it the notion of doing good to or for someone.

TO EDUCATE IS TO IMPROVE SOMEONE

"To educate," Peters says, functions logically like the expression "to reform." It does not make sense to say that I "reformed" someone, but did not do him any good. "Befriend" is another word of the same kind. One cannot "befriend" without helping in some way. Webster's *New World Dictionary* defines education as "the process of training and developing the knowledge, skill, mind, character, etc., especially by formal schooling; teaching; training." This standard usage supports Peters' contention. "It would be a logical contradiction," he writes, "to say that a man had been educated but that he had in no way changed for the better. . . ."[1]

From the proposition "X educated Y," we may draw two conclusions: (1) Y was educated, and (2) Y was changed for the better

---

[1] R. S. Peters, "What Is an Educational Process?" in R. S. Peters (ed.), *The Concept of Education*, p. 4.

in X's (and perhaps Y's) judgment. This final qualification is important. "To educate" means to intend something good for the student, and to achieve that intended good, but it may not be good. All we are saying, then, is that the good achieved is good by the educator's standard.

On this basis, the punitive jailer may produce some good in his prisoner, but he cannot qualify as an educator because he intends only to punish. But the educator with a mistaken notion of good, who wholeheartedly undertakes his task with this notion in mind, does qualify.

Thus, the Stalinist schoolmaster may qualify as an educator provided he is sincere in his belief that Stalinism is good. He may teach Lysenko's mistaken views of biology, and spoil his student's ability to solve problems in that science, but if he is convinced that he is doing the right thing he is *educating* in our sense. Any criticism of him in his role as educator would have to be directed at his mistaken notions of biology, not at his intentions as an educator.

This does not seem to get us very far until we remember that the educator aims at *understanding*, and understanding is a self-correcting factor in human life. Thus, it is commonly complained that our prisons are schools of crime, that the inmates are taught criminality. Is that good? We might reply somewhat as follows. To come to understand something, say, safecracking or new ways to commit crimes, is not in itself bad. Even the guardians of the peace study such things. What is missing in prison is a broad understanding of the meaning of criminal acts, and this must be counted as a deficiency of education. Thus, to understand something bad, like how to commit crimes, is not itself bad. What is bad is the disposition to employ it for bad ends. It is not what the prisoner understands that is bad, but the deficiency of his understanding in those areas appropriate to the application of those skills to social life.

Consider the case of so-called Nazi education during the Hitler regime. Could we say that this was *educating*? In one use of the word we would have to agree. It certainly is standard usage to refer to the "Nazi system of education," just as an historian might refer to Greek or medieval education. On closer viewing, we could, I believe, set up the following criteria to test whether the schoolmasters Nazis were *educating*: (1) The Nazi educator must believe that

Nazi doctrines are true. Lying would not count as educating. (2) The Nazi educator must sincerely believe that teaching these beliefs to students was doing them some good. (3) The Nazi educator must use methods consistent with teaching. He must not merely indoctrinate or condition his students, nor may he employ threats of imprisonment and torture to obtain their consent to his doctrine. (4) The Nazi educator must appeal to understanding in some broad sense.

It is generally agreed that at least on counts three and four, Nazi educators were miserably lacking. In the light of this, would we say that Nazi school men *educated* their students? I think not. What we are forced to say, then, is that the Nazi system of education failed to educate. If they had taught their students to understand the Jewish situation, they would have found their prejudices dissolving. In this, as with other major tenets of the system of Nazi beliefs, they would not have dared open the classroom to the free exchange of rational criticism that lies at the heart of teaching. Nor, we are told, did they do so.

Let me clarify what I am saying. I am not denying that the Nazis may have been justified in their handling of educational problems. Opinions on that score are irrelevant at this point. What I am saying is that having handled them in that way disqualifies allowing what they did to count as *educating*.

The standard meaning of *educating* has emerged in the long centuries of western civilization. It has come to mean, I think, what might be called a rational initiation into the spheres of civilized meaning. If what the Nazis did with their educational system had become standard for western society, the concept of *educating* would have gradually been forgotten, and *indoctrination* or *propaganda* would have taken its place.

Let me summarize the argument so far: (1) Educating is doing some good for someone, at least in the opinion of the educator. (2) Educating is engendering meanings through understanding. (3) Understanding, unlike propaganda or indoctrination, is a self-correcting notion (as in science where false notions are fated to be disproven).

If we were to add a fourth proposition, (4) engendering meanings through awakening understanding is *good*, then we could logically conclude that, therefore, (5) educating is good. An argument for proposition (6) would entail the attempt to establish rational grounds for a value-claim. Many philosophers believe that rational grounds cannot be discovered for values. We will discuss such matters in a later chapter. Here we must be content with a lesser claim, namely, that if (1) educating is doing some good for someone at least in the opinion of the educator, and (2) educating is engendering meanings through awakening understanding, then (3) anyone who engenders meanings through awakening understanding is doing something that he believes to be *good*. The educator has made a commitment to the proposition that "educating is good" by undertaking his role as an educator. In other words, the *goodness* of the task of educating is a presupposition of deciding to undertake that task.

WHAT IS UNDERSTANDING?

We have used the word *understanding* throughout the preceding discussion. Some comments about it are in order. The first thing to clarify is that though the meaning of understanding varies with the subject matter understood, this variation is well within the limits of a single family of meanings. I may, for instance, *understand* a work of art, the rationale of a moral act, or an explanation in physics. What I understand in each of these examples is controlled by what could be called a distinct *logic* or *rationale*. I prefer the word *logos* in this connection because it has a wider significance than the other two words. It would seem odd, for instance, to speak of the "logic" of a work of art, but since I want to say something like that I will use "logos" instead.

Men understand, in some proper sense of that word, the moral rightness of an action, the beauty of a painting, the fitness of a religious ritual, the grace of a ballet, or the validity of a solution to a mathematical problem. We can see the difference in the logos of these areas of understanding when we ask for relevant reasons to support such judgments.

There are reasons for saying that an act is moral or that a scientific explanation is true, but they are different kinds of reasons. When one knows the reasons appropriate to that mode of understanding, he can be said to understand the logos of the subject under consideration. When certain features of a building are pointed out to a person who appreciates architecture, he can see some of the reasons why the structure under consideration is right aesthetically. The reasons that one wants, in connection with moral actions, may be an elucidation of general principles, say, the principle of universality or the establishment of relevant facts.

One of the major meanings of being educated is to have some grasp of this range of reasons, the scope of certain ways of understanding. This saves our definition of education from being too cerebral. When Hutchins says that education has something to do with the mind, he is no doubt correct. The word "mind" suggests too intellectual a notion of understanding. The broader significance that I have attributed to it seem more faithful to our general use of the term.

In summary, we can say that activity we call "educating" is an initiation into the sphere of understanding in its multidimensionality. It is to grasp the logos of the range of civilized meanings.

MUST AN EDUCATOR HAVE AN AIM?

In a celebrated essay titled as this subheading, Peters raises the important issue of whether means-end language is really appropriate in talking about education.[2] Educational theory is replete with discussions of so-called goals, aims, and purposes of education along with suggested means to these ends. Peters contends that the means-end model implicit in this *aim* language is misleading. If we believe that everything that educators do is best considered as a means to some extrinsic end, does that illuminate or obscure the meaning of education? I agree with Peters that it tends to obscure it. If, as I have argued, education is an initiation into the realms of human meaning, a coming to understand, then education is essentially one of the great ends of life, not merely a means to an end.

To be sure, like other human ends, such as love or beauty, for

---

[2] R. A. Peters, *Authority, Responsibility and Education* (New York: Atherton Press, 1966), pp. 83–95.

instance, understanding may be useful and work salutary effects in the total economy of existence, but to consider it merely as a means will only tend to obscure its nature. That is to say, coming to understanding is so central to the enterprise of being human that it belongs to the realm of ends. To be moral, to appreciate art and literature, and to perceive the natural world in its organized intricacy— all these are possible only with understanding—indeed, are forms of understanding, modes of participation in humane meanings. The very substance of human action, says Peters, "is inseparable, too, from the concept of 'knowing what we are doing'."[3]

It would be better, he suggests, to understand that "many disputes about the aims of education are disputes about principles of procedure rather than about 'aims' in the sense of objectives to be arrived at by taking appropriate means."[4]

He cites as example the dispute over the derivation of the word *education*. Those who claim that its proper derivation is from the Latin *educere*, "to lead out," say that the *aim* of education is to develop the potentialities of individuals. This might be better expressed by saying that "leading out" is one of the best ways to achieve understanding. "To lead out" is, then, the means rather than the end. Moreover, the particular "leading out" that is germane to education—the contribution that educators can make to "leading out" which is distinct from what parents, friends, counselors, and others may do—is to patiently work with the growing understanding of the student as an end in itself. The educational program entailed in the concept of *leading the student out* does suggest that methods of teaching might be more closely oriented to the growing understanding of the pupil than to the achieved knowledge of the teacher. There is no question that this may help in the search for the best way to bring about education itself. This transposes the realization of the student's potential from the status of an end to the status of a means, making education what it should be, an end in itself.

The same can be said of other so-called *aims* of education: to reconstruct society, to shape moral character, to promote growth, to

3 *Ibid.*, p. 123.
4 *Ibid.*, p. 90.

initiate the young into an ongoing culture, and so on. All of these aims are germane to education, but they are not best considered on the model of aims. These so-called aims prove to be values or programs suitable to a good society or a good life. Insofar as they are wise, they must be taken into account by educators in considering how to perform their tasks, but they do not in themselves define what it is to educate.

Aims, like the above, arise in societies at certain junctures of history. They are thrown up by a society's traditions and values, or by its own vision of the good life or a good society. At creative periods of history, they are projected in vivid form by the visionaries of a culture. Thus, at the present moment in America, for example, we have become acutely aware of the value of preparing human beings to participate democratically in the institutions that shape their lives.

The relationship between the activity of educating and these aims is complex and important. Several of them should be noted. The first has already been suggested, namely, that an aim may clarify the procedures that educators might consider in educating. The notion of democratic participation is an example. The educator may be well advised to examine the degree to which such a policy of participation may enhance learning, and even open up new dimensions of meaning to be grasped by the participants.

Another example of this potential effect upon education are proposals that educators should shape moral character, reconstruct society, or initiate students into an appreciation of the arts. Although these do not in themselves define educating, they cast a strong light on the process. They tend to open up new areas for educational activity. Education, in its basic sense, has a natural affinity to an intellectualism that often biases education toward subject matters with clear cognitive significance. Claims, such as those just mentioned, tend to open a new inquiry into the rationale of morality, social change, or art.

This suggests a second relationship between the proposed *aims* and education. Educating is not consistent with all styles of social organization and purpose. If a society opts for values that are inconsistent with educating, the enterprise of education will languish. I have argued that this happened in Germany under the Nazis. By making anti-Semitism and a blind obedience to the leader dominant social values, they automatically, to the same degree, denigrated education. Indoctrination in race prejudice and obedience to orders both stand in flat contradiction to the activity of educating. A paranoid society will, in the nature of the case, find education a poor companion and will inevitably seek a substitute.

It should be apparent that social aims, if they are wise, contribute to the educational process, and the educational process, if it is faithful to itself, will contribute to social aims. However, neither of these facts is adequate to define clearly just what the activity of educating really is.

These remarks would be incomplete without reference to Whitehead's celebrated book, *The Aims of Education*.[5] I have no inclination to deny that this work of a great and influential philosopher contains many reflections of importance to educators. The point of the preceding criticisms is one of terminology, not of substance. What I am saying is that what Whitehead calls "aims" might better be considered as *means* or methods of educating. For instance, his suggestion about the three stages of the educational process— romance, precision, and generalization—can claim to be good accounts of how understanding grows. This is different than speaking of them as the *aims* of understanding.

[5] Alfred North Whitehead, *The Aims of Education* (New York: Macmillan, 1929).

8

TEACHING PROPOSALS

Just about everybody seems to feel called upon to tell teachers how
they should teach, not only scholars but journalists, politicians,
businessmen, and students. Analysts believe that philosophers in
their role as philosophers have no special competence in this matter.
But in their role as the logical conscience of the community, they
insist on the right to ask anyone who makes educational proposals,
either in regard to teaching or the curriculum, questions like these:
"What do you mean?" "What do you presuppose about knowledge,
value, learning, man, and society?" "What kinds of reasons can be
given for your proposals?" "What would you need to know, or what
values would you need to approve in order to validate your proposal?"

THE SERVICE OF PHILOSOPHY

Since philosophers are often charged with their alleged uselessness, let us consider further the services philosophy could render teachers and curriculum builders. (1) Philosophy can clarify what is logically implied in educational proposals. Here is a sample of the kinds of issues that philosophy can serve to clarify: (a) In the business of teaching, it can elucidate what it means to teach for "behavioral outcomes," or show the relationship between the notion of *operant conditioning* and the concept of teaching. (b) Curricula do not just happen, they are *chosen*. To choose always presupposes a complex tissue of *values* (that make the choice good), facts (that constitute *evidence* for the alleged wisdom of the choice), and *presuppositions* about the nature of man and society. Frankena's chart, examined in Chapter 3, outlines the logical priority of these questions.

To be sure, a great number of school practices, both pedagogical and curricular, are the result of quasi-political pressure from the community. Presumably, the community debates these matters before the choices are made. Philosophers can serve as critics of the kinds of arguments used by both sides in these debates.

(2) Another service that philosophy can render is to explore the rationale of given bodies of curricular subject matter. If this rationale is concealed from the teacher, it is unlikely to become known to the learner. If it is unknown to the curriculum planner, his curriculum will lack coherence and become a mere ad hoc cafeteria of items with no inner relationships. Philosophers have labored long and diligently over such topics as the philosophy of science, art, history, law, religion, moral behavior (ethics), social systems, education, and so on. Every subject that can be *taught* is a realm of quasi-unique meanings that deserve analysis, or belongs to a class of subjects that together make up such a realm.

(3) A related service of philosophy is its contribution to the integration of the curriculum by clarifying the rationale of *clusters* of subjects. It can, for example, offer analyses of meanings common to the art, literature, and music of a period, showing their interrelationships. The same can be done for the political, social, and economic thought of a period.

(4) Finally, I suspect that philosophy might be of help in

clarifying the relationship of certain aspects of the curriculum to social and personal values, and to the overall styles of life to which they logically belong.

TEACHING FOR BEHAVIORAL OUTCOMES

What is actually being proposed to teachers when they are told to teach for *behavioral outcomes?* This is not the same question as, "What is the technique involved in teaching for behavioral outcomes?" We are concerned not with how it is done but with what it *means.* We have already discussed many topics, like conditioning, which are relevant to this discussion. Since teaching for behavioral outcomes is urged so vigorously in some educational circles, it will be worthwhile considering it from several new angles.

First of all, since many of my remarks will be critical, I want to make it clear that there is no philosophical reason for opposing many features of this proposal. It seems reasonable enough that teachers should ask themselves afresh what they are trying to do, and to consider what kinds of evidence they look for in their students to show that they have in some measure succeeded.

There are, however, several serious ambiguities in the proposal.

(1) Teaching for behavioral outcomes is a means-end scheme of the sort criticized earlier. It suggests that teaching is a means, that what goes on in the classroom is of value only in terms of some terminal behavior. There is no reason to repeat this earlier argument here.

(2) A means-end scheme suggests that any means which succeeds in attaining a desired behavior may be a useful teaching technique. We have seen that this is not so. Scheffler makes the point quite clearly: "Behavior may be effectively brought into accord with norms through threats, hypnosis, bribery, drugs, lies, suggestions, and open force. Teaching may, to be sure, proceed by various methods, but some ways of getting people to do things are excluded from the standard range of the term 'teaching'."[1]

---

[1] Israel Scheffler, "The Concept of Teaching," in Macmillan and Nelson (eds.), *Concepts of Teaching: Philosophical Essays*, p. 17.

(3) Some learning, perhaps the most important learning, has no definite behavioral equivalent. We have discussed this point before, but let us consider a further example provided by Scheffler. Suppose we ask what "work on a geometry problem" means behaviorally. To work on a geometry problem means not only that the student is doing something observable (writing, reading, figuring, and so on), but that he is also thinking. Trying involves thinking. To judge, writes Scheffler, "that he is thinking is already to go beyond his manifest bodily movement. . . ."[2] None of his behavior —pacing, staring out the window, scratching on the pad of paper— is "either a necessary or sufficient condition of such working."[3]

On might object that we do not know at the time whether the student is working on the problem, but we will know when we ask him to perform mathematically later. This does not improve the case. To be sure, if we present a proof and ask that the student repeat it, we have behavioral evidence that he can indeed report this proof. Is this doing mathematics? If he understands mathematics, he will be able to do many things—even invent new proofs— that have no behavioral equivalents. Scheffler points out that we cannot characterize the production of proofs in advance. There is, he says, no "pattern of speaking or writing movements [that] constitutes a sufficient condition for problem-solution in geometry or mathematics."[4] This is also true in science. When theories have been once presented, they must be evaluated. Since we have "no general rules for the production of worth-while theories," Scheffler writes, "to think of problem solving as a complex of sequences of movements governed by rule is thus a myth."[5] We must agree with his conclusion that "attempts to think of teaching in extreme behavioristic terms are, at best, ambiguous and at worst, totally misguided."[6]

Not to belabor the case, but another example may help clarify this important point. Robert H. Ennis has attempted to define "critical thinking" in behavioral terms. At the end of his long essay

[2] *Ibid.*, p. 25.
[3] *Ibid.*
[4] *Ibid.*, p. 26.
[5] *Ibid.*
[6] *Ibid.*

in which he has listed scores of criteria for various aspects of critical thinking, an essay that incidentally contains many valuable ideas, he warns that "these criteria must be applied with discretion; they are not to be applied mechanically."[7] This he says is partly due to the need for brevity, but also "partly because a list of exception and qualifications would be endless, if we were to attempt to list them all. . . ."[8] These qualifications give away his case. Of course, there are "endless qualifications" because critical thinking cannot be formulated in strict behavioral terms.

(4) In the light of these considerations, it becomes clear that behavioral equivalents are lacking for all but the most elementary skills. Even in these cases, the student's performance may not be all he has learned or even the most important part of what he has learned. A master teacher of a skill will convey to the student an understanding of the principles underlying that skill. At an early stage, though he may have learned these principles well, he may not perform in any way commensurate with them. He may, in fact, spend the rest of his life improving his performance using the principles involved. However, there may be no single point where the student's understanding of those principles is manifested fully in behavior. Consider, for example, a pianist who, having studied with a master teacher, goes on perfecting his playing throughout his career by means of the understanding conveyed years earlier to him by his teacher. All this is even more true of areas like the study of humane letters where there is no visible performance.

(5) The proposal that teachers aim at behavioral goals leads to a substitution of a by-product for the real goal. In teaching Shakespeare, for instance, it would seem reasonable to want to arouse in the student an understanding and appreciation of his works. The student's behavior is a by-product that may be useful in sampling his progress in the essential matter. If the teacher sets up, for instance, as a goal the student's performance on a test or his writing of an essay, and so on, the teacher may find himself simply supplying the answers to set questions or giving

[7] Robert H. Ennis, "A Concept of Critical Thinking," in Komisar and Macmillan (eds.), *Psychological Concepts in Education*, p. 143.
[8] *Ibid.*

information easily useful for writing the essay. Is this teaching Shakespeare?

Reports about the system of higher education in India suggest the kind of educational deterioration that can take place. There, it is said that no instructor dare deviate from the routine of reading the answers to possible questions on the state examinations. The behavior desired is the passing of these exams. The strict adherence to this goal tends to empty university courses of all attempts to understand or appreciate what is being taught. Unfortunately, something like this seems to take place everywhere when certification becomes a goal rather than a by-product or sign of some other achievement. It would seem to be hard enough to avoid this result at best, to say nothing of making a virtue of aiming at that which is not the prime meaning of teaching.

(6) This proposal belongs to a questionable trend in modern life, namely, to substitute technique for human involvement. Ordinary language is replete with terms of negative evaluation for this technicizing when it becomes overly successful: the *legalist* who somehow abuses the law with legal technicalities; the *moralist* who substitutes dead rules for the ethical spirit; the *pietist* who does the same in religion; the *technician* whose musical performance is correct but dead. "The letter kills but the spirit gives life."[9]

(7) The criteria for selecting behavioral equivalents lie in a nonbehavioral realm, that is, we must know what it means to *understand* mathematics or to *appreciate* music, for instance, before we can set up plausible behavioral tests of that understanding. It is this nonbehavioral understanding that gives unity and order to the proposed behavioral equivalents.

Nonbehavioral understanding is also what gives coherence to a course or a curriculum One junior high school faculty came up with 3500 different behavioral equivalents. We may ask whether it makes more sense to substitute these hundreds of behavioral objectives for the course or department names that now describe the content of education.

I once worked out the *behavioral objectives* for a course in philosophy of education. I divided the behaviors into two groups: (1)

[9] 2 Cor. 3:6.

those relevant to knowledge *about philosophy*, and (2) those relevant to *doing philosophy*. In the first group, I put such items as: (1) Give an accurate account, oral or written, of the various competing notions regarding the nature of philosophy: global, analytic, Marxist, pragmatist, and existentialist. (2) Give an accurate account of some of the major concepts of the philosophers who have written on education themes: Whitehead, Plato, Rousseau, and Kant. In the second group concerned with *doing philosophy*, I listed such items as: (1) Write a coherent analysis in linguistic terms of some major concepts in education: *teaching, learning,* and *conditioning.* (2) Engage in a critical philosophical dialogue making the various moves that are characteristic of philosophical argument.

After I had finished my list, I found myself asking what my *real objectives* were, objectives for which there were no strict behavioral equivalents. I listed such items as: (1) To understand the meaning of the philosophical enterprise and to begin to appreciate its goal of rational clarity. (2) To come to believe that the unexamined life is not worth living. (3) To begin to develop a taste for philosophic discussion in reading and talking. (4) To apply philosophic criteria to one's own actions, thought, beliefs, arguments, and judgments. (5) To come to understand what it means to teach, to educate, to be a teacher-educator, and to prize that calling for the right reasons.

PROGRAMMED LEARNING

Programmed learning is another widely popular teaching proposal. There are two aspects of this proposal that should be sorted out: (1) breaking learning down into easy steps, and (2) the reenforcement of the learner's correct responses. The first item is clearly related to the essentials of teaching, and is highly relevant to any effort to teach for understanding. The second involves a number of issues that need clarification. Reenforcement is a concept from the psychological theory of operant conditioning. All of the previous remarks on conditioning are relevant at this point, and it would be tedious to repeat them, but there is one question that we have not asked, namely, what is the role of reenforcement in teaching and educating. The hungry rat's behavior is reenforced by being given food. As I have pointed out, this could not count as a teaching method.

Compare two possible cases: (1) The child receives a piece of candy from the teaching machine every time he gives a correct response, and (2) the child enjoys the satisfaction of having got the right answer, or the satisfaction of having come to understand some aspect of the material. The first case is innocent enough at certain levels with very young and, perhaps, with mentally or emotionally handicapped children. If this method were continued into later years, the student would have learned, among other things, that the rewards of learning are entirely extrinsic. To some extent, we have done this with our present system of grades and honors. If educating is getting people to understand and disposed to behave in modes appropriate to that understanding, then there comes an upper limit in the age to which this method is suitable. Just what the effects of extrinsic reward reenforcement may be is an empirical matter worthy of study, but there is the lively danger that what may be learned is how to use approved social behavior (in this case performing educational tasks) to get extrinsic rewards. Such learning is contrary to the notion of becoming humanely educated.

READINESS

Many teaching proposals include reference to the so-called readiness of the student. In spite of its apparent simplicity, this concept proves to be complex. When you ask whether a student is "ready" to master a given subject matter, you are not asking for evidence about something he has done, but something he is able to do. Robert Ennis suggests that we call this "capacital readiness." Capacital readiness is itself two-pronged. It refers to both biological maturation and to predisposing social experience.

The French psychologist Piaget has enjoyed a renewed popularity of his ideas dealing with the stages of pupil readiness. His exploration of the different ways in which the rules of marble games are viewed by boys of different ages is a good example. Studies of this kind lend a statistical probability to the judgment that a child of a given age is ready to understand certain ideas.

But *normal* biological maturation alone does not satisfy all the criteria of readiness. The child's social environment must have contained opportunities for experiences of certain sorts or he will not be ready in spite of his physical maturation. Fortunately a judgment concerning the student's capacital readiness can be made with a relatively high degree of probability on the basis of psychological and sociological studies of groups typical of that student.

There is still the problem of what Ennis calls *dispositional* readiness. A disposition, we saw earlier, is not like *capacital* readiness. The glass that has the capacity to shatter under a given blow cannot be said to have a disposition to shatter in this way. Human readiness includes something like an *interest* in, or a desire for, a certain new idea.

The prediction of dispositional readiness differs from capacital readiness in that predictions concerning it are never strictly verifiable. If, for instance, we decide that a student is ready in the dispositional sense to study a given subject, and his teachers do not succeed in teaching it to him, we are not justified in saying that he was not ready. He may have been ready, but the teaching may have been inept. Of course, if the teaching succeeds, we may indeed say that the student was ready. This is not very useful, however, since the whole idea of readiness is supposed to help the educator decide when to introduce a given topic. It is difficult, as Ennis says, to "deny conclusively that a subject is ready for mastery."[10] Unless something can be known in advance about the readiness of the pupil, the concept cannot serve as a guide. This empirical ambiguity should serve as a warning to the educator who takes the social scientist's recommendation regarding *readiness* too simplistically.

Pointing out the ambiguity in the notion of *readiness* may be useful educationally in suggesting that we can never be sure we have assessed student readiness correctly. Jerome Bruner's proposals

[10] Robert H. Ennis, "Readiness to Master a Principle," in Komisar and Macmillan (eds.), *Psychological Concepts in Education*, p. 143.

concerning the *spiral* curriculum (discussed in the next chapter) contain some surprising notions about the very early readiness, both capacital and dispositional, to grasp concepts fundamental to more advanced and sophisticated subject matters.

EXPERIENCE

Teachers are often advised that their students will learn best from *experience*. No doubt, everyone learns from experience, but without considerable clarification this advice is not of much use to the educator. The teacher must know what *experience* means in the teaching context. The experiences of prison may be educational, but they cannot count as teaching. The teacher is concerned with the student's coming to understand something, and it is in this context that *experience* must be defined. Undoubtedly, the exhortation to appeal to *experience* is directed against the practice of mere verbalization or *telling*, and we have already seen that *telling* is not the whole of teaching.

Several things need to be clarified. (1) Mere sensation, seeing, touching, and testing, cannot count as *experience* in teaching. To be useful educationally, sensations have to be enjoyed within a context of meaning. The sensory experience that the teacher is interested in is one that has a meaning related to the subject matter he wants the student to understand. This means that an appeal to experience is not a panacea, nor is it easy. *Experiences* can be as meaningless (and boring) as mere words.

The appeal to experience requires a judicious sampling of sensations that will appear to the student as an "illustration" of the verbal instruction, that is, the experience must be structured just as the instruction must be structured.

I have said an "illustration" of the verbal instruction because it is manifestly impossible to experience everything essential. Concepts outrun experience in every field. Experiences can only serve as crucial examples, not as substitutes for concepts.

It was considerations of this kind that led Dewey to criticize the notion of *experience in general*, and to talk about it in the context of problem solving. Both experiences and theory become significant to the student, according to Dewey, when they are focused in problem to be solved. Every experience has a meaning in its context, and every theory suggests a structure within which it is possible to discover a solution. Because problem solving has a kind of rationale of its own, Dewey, was able to speak intelligibly of *an experience* rather than *experience in general*. *An experience* has a beginning, middle, and end, beginning with muddled and confused features and gradually crystalizing in the final solution.

Another way of structuring experience is the *demonstration*. Teaching through demonstration requires not merely showing the students something, it means illustrating something. A demonstration is set or ordered to a point; it arranges specific experiences directed to specific understandings.

The concept of *implicit* knowledge, suggested by Michael Polanyi, a British philosopher of science, can help us here. Just as we have pointed out that it is impossible to *experience* everything, he argues that it is impossible to *say* everything. Verbal instruction is intelligible only against a background of *implicit* knowledge. Since there are things that cannot be told, the experience of *apprenticeship* is important. The student watches and imitates. He gradually becomes initiated into those implicit understandings that cannot be explicated in words. Imagine, for instance, a primitive Australian trying to assemble a mail-order wheelbarrow guided only by written instructions. Not knowing either what a wheelbarrow looks like or what it is used for, he would lack *implicit* understanding of the artifact to be assembled. If he succeeds, it would no doubt take weeks of experimentation, but more probably he would give up in despair. Nor would it help much to expand the written instructions. The attempt to fill in everything necessary to a person so lacking in implicit knowledge would make for a confusing multiplicity of details.

It is this factor of *implicit* knowledge that accounts for the difference between the mechanical skills of developing countries and those which have enjoyed generations of engineers. In the early stages of development, these countries turn out mere imitations, often bad ones, of models designed elsewhere. Usually by the third generation, when young students can serve as apprentices to former apprentices, they go beyond imitation to inventiveness. The difference between the quality of goods now manufactured in Japan and those produced before World War II is an example of this change.

It should be apparent, then, that the concept of *learning by experience* is not as simple as it first appeared.

TEACHING BY PARTICIPATION

The concept of apprenticeship suggests another proposal for teaching, that of participation. According to this proposal, the teacher and student become coparticipants in the activity of learning. This is highly consistent with what we have seen to be the paradigmatic sense of *teaching* and the essential meaning of *educating*. There are several reasons why this is so. First, the teacher undertakes his task with the hope of developing understanding on the part of his student, but he cannot guarantee this result. He has to wait for something to happen on the student's side. The closer he is to the student in the learning enterprise the more likely this response will take place.

Second, the teacher is always accountable to the student for his reasoning. His position as teacher is due solely to his superior training and experience, but this does not make him infallible. In most cases, he will be learning along with the student. The student can appeal to reason and evidence over the teacher's word, and the teacher must submit to that appeal. Some teachers feel that this imperils their status and threatens teaching effectiveness, but if everyone understands what teaching is this need not be the case. The degree to which the teacher seeks refuge in his professional status marks the degree to which he has stopped teaching and begun to indoctrinate.

EVALUATION

What is presupposed by the system of examinations, grades, and degrees? On the one hand, there is nothing inconsistent between this system and educating, provided evaluation is interpreted consistently and used as a way of sampling the progress of the student. Under such a regime, the student might well ask for testing to see if he is on the right track. There is, however, another use of evaluation that is inconsistent with educating, or at least in a high degree of tension with it. That is where educators and students alike come to look upon the grades and degrees as the primary aim or reward of instruction. This view suffers from all the objections that we found in teaching for *behavioral consequences*. In fact, high performance on evaluating scales is often looked upon as the desired goal of teaching and learning.

A defense of evaluation can be mounted from the perspective of social necessity. Competence, it is argued, must often be certified so that able people are selected for medicine, law, teaching, and so on. This makes evaluative schemes in the form of credits and degrees even more of a prize and therefore more likely to become the reason for undertaking a course of study. Philosophy is not the discipline to work out the most viable answer to this puzzle, but it can offer the educator a salutary warning of the conflict in concepts involved.

Having sampled an analysis of some of the concepts inherent in various teaching proposals, let us now do the same for suggestions regarding curricula.

9

CURRICULAR PROPOSALS

Today's educator must feel somewhat overwhelmed by the flood of curricular demands made on the schools. Philosophy cannot determine which of these may best deserve implementation, but it can help to clarify what they *mean*. Some of the concepts central to these proposals are part of the standard vocabulary of education while others, like *confluent education*, have revolutionary implications. It makes sense to invoke a mood of philosophical detachment long enough to get our bearings.

THE CLAIM OF "GENERATIVE" SUBJECT MATTER

The popular press often urges educators to get back to the three R's. In its simplistic form, such a demand need not be considered seriously. It may, however, serve to raise the question of whether there is such a thing as basic subject matter. We have seen that teaching is a triadic affair which includes something taught, but this does not settle *what* should be taught.

One answer to the question of what should be taught is so-called generative subject matter. Generative subjects are those that are so fundamental to education that they appear at every level and are a precondition of nearly everything else. Certainly, the three R's can claim something of that status, the development of some minimal competence in the symbols of thought and expression: speaking, reading, writing, and reasoning.

Concern for generative subject matter is part of a larger proposal made by Jerome Bruner in his *The Process of Education*. He makes two significant claims: (1) Learning at early stages, he says, "should not only take us somewhere; it should allow us later to go further more easily."[1] (2) Young students are fundamentally interested in and able to understand the logos of adult subject matter. These are, of course, psychological not philosophical claims, but they fit with many of the things we have already noted about the meaning of "teaching" and "educating."

The fault of old-fashioned, adult-subject-oriented education Dewey and other progressive educators have criticized was that it allowed for Bruner's first proposition, but rejected or did not understand the second. Consequently, educators faced a dilemma: On the one hand, the student needed to learn certain things in order to become a knowledgeable adult, and, on the other, the student was not interested nor was he ready to grasp these subjects. The teacher was compelled to become an authoritarian indoctrinator. This posture made the educator vulnerable to the criticism of the progressives who seemed to bespeak the child's real nature. The trouble

[1] Jerome S. Bruner, *The Process of Education* (New York: Vintage Books, 1960), p. 17.

with many childish interests is that they are temporary, and they do not carry the educational process forward. Pandering to them often resulted in making education into a kind of entertainment.

If Bruner is correct, this dilemma can be overcome. Children, he says, *are* interested in understanding adult subjects, and, moreover, they can grasp them if the child's intuitive mode of thought is understood, and if instruction is oriented to that mode of understanding. This is how he puts it:

> The early teaching of science, mathematics, social studies, and literature should be designed to teach these subjects with scrupulous intellectual honesty, but with an emphasis upon the intuitive grasp of ideas and upon the use of these basic ideas. A curriculum as it develops should revisit these basic ideas repeatedly, building upon them until the student has grasped the full formal apparatus that goes with them.[2]

This is what he calls the "spiral curriculum."

I have argued that the fundamental meaning of "educating" is the initiation of the student into the realm of human meanings. Bruner's research on the spiral curriculum makes this enterprise more practically plausible than most of the work done on the psychology of the curriculum prior to his time. If the child can indeed grasp in an intuitive way the logos of materials that he will need to know as an adult, and, if, further, he is interested in understanding these things, then, the whole business is put on a more substantial footing. The claims of generative subject matter can now be considered without falling back into an authoritarian approach that ignores the child's own way of learning. Instead of endless drill and rote learning, the young student can be really *taught* in the paradigmatic sense of the word. Hence, what he is taught will become more significant to him as he moves through the schools. The psychological point is that children are curious. They enjoy learning as such. The teacher need not stay with trifling interests because the pupil is young. Even at the tenderest age, his powers of understanding are unfolding, and he not only derives great satisfaction, but also sustains an enduring interest in exercising them.

It will still, no doubt, be true that the ratio of training to teaching will be higher in the early years than in the later ones, but

---

[2] *Ibid.*

appeals to understanding will never be absent. As the student matures, the teacher's role will gradually move from being a director of the learning process to that of a facilitator of learning. Ideally, at the end of the period of formal schooling, the student will be ready to learn on his own.

Bruner's work finds confirmation in the work of Benjamin Bloom and his associates in their two-volume work on the *Taxonomy of Educational Objectives*.[3] These volumes offer an analysis of the natural sequence of learning in both cognitive and affective areas. We shall consider later the question of affective education. Here we are concerned with the authors' conception of the sequence of learning from the simplest levels of understanding to the most comprehensive.

The *sequence* in cognitive learning, they claim, is as follows: (1) Knowledge of specifics: terminology and facts. (2) Knowledge of ways and means of dealing with specifics: organizing, studying, judging, and criticizing. These include (a) an early awareness of conventional terminology and methods for dealing with specifics, awareness of trends and sequences, such as the continuity and development of American culture; (b) knowledge of classifications and categories used in given subject fields; (c) knowledge of criteria by which facts, principles, opinions, and conduct are tested or judged; and (d) knowledge of methods of inquiry in such fields. (3) Knowledge of the universals and abstractions in a field: This involves knowledge of the major schemes and patterns by which phenomena and ideas are organized.

From another perspective, Bloom considers knowledge in terms of intellectual abilities and skills. The competences are traced *developmentally* as follows: (1) Comprehension as the lowest level of understanding (2) Application: the use of abstractions in particular and concrete situations. (3) Analysis: the constitutent elements or parts of any hierarchy of ideas are clarified. (4) Synthesis: the putting together of elements and parts so as to form a whole. (5) Evaluation: the development of standards of appraisal, both internal and external, appropriate to the scheme involved.

[3] Benjamin S. Bloom, *et al.*, *Taxonomy of Educational Objectives*, Handbook I: *Cognitive Domain*; Handbook II: *Affective Domain* (New York: McKay , 1956, 1964).

The significance of the *Taxonomy* is that it spells out both the inner structure of understanding and the outer structure of symbolic systems. This makes clearer the meaning of educating in our sense.

A final word on the subject matter content of education. Present-day educators are under pressure to think of education in terms of personal development, social relationships, and so on. This claim is important and will be studied presently. However, the cognitive dimension is, as we shall see, a kind of special property of schools and universities. Without it, affective education would be a truncated affair.

Michael Oakeshott, in an essay on "Learning and Teaching," eloquently bespeaks this point:

> . . . this inheritance is an historic achievement . . . it is what human beings have achieved . . . by exploiting the opportunities of fortune and by means of their own efforts. It comprises the standards of conduct to which from time to time they have given their preferences, the pro- and con-feelings to which they have given their approval and disapproval, the intellectual enterprises they have happened upon and pursued, the duties they have imposed upon themselves, the activities they have delighted in, the hopes they have entertained and the disappointments they have suffered. . . .
>
> A teacher, then, engaged in initiating his pupils into so contingent an inheritance, might be excused for thinking that he needs some assurance of its worth. For, like many of us, he may be expected to have a superstitious prejudice against the human race and to be satisfied only when he can feel himself anchored to something for which human beings are not responsible. But he must be urged to have the courage of his circumstances. This man-made inheritance contains everything to which value may be attributed; it is the ground and context of every judgment of better or worse. . . . He may be excused if he finds the present dominant image of civilized life too disagreeable to impart with any enthusiasm to his pupils. But if he has no confidence in any of the standards of worth written into this inheritance of human achievement, he had better not be a teacher; he would have nothing to teach.[4]

Oakeshott knows that the individual teacher cannot deal with this entire body of civilized meanings, but his rationale as a teacher lies within it. Learning is always related to, if not exclusively identified with, an historic inheritance, and "that what is

---

[4] Michael Oakeshott, "Learning and Teaching," in R. S. Peters (ed.), *The Concept of Education*, p. 162.

to be handed on and learned, known and understood, are thoughts and various 'expressions' of thoughts."[5]

The above remarks about subject matter raise other questions. One of them is suggested by concept of *relevance*.

RELEVANCE

There is a great cry today for *relevance* in the curriculum. What does this mean? Presumably, it means relevance to the student's needs, interests, and so on. We will look briefly at needs and interests, but, I think that the more basic meaning of *relevance* is that the student be able to see the value or significance of what he is studying. It is too easy a solution for the educator to arrange a curriculum around the subjects in which the student is immediately interested. Such a curriculum is in danger of being irrelevant in the larger sense; when the youthful interest has changed, all he has learned is outmoded. To short circuit the search for relevance by orienting everything to job finding or social success, and so on, is to eventually sell the student short.

Generative subject matter, leading to initiation into the realm of human meanings, has few rivals in its claim for relevance. Language, for instance, is relevant to almost every interest that will emerge throughout life. Failure to master the symbols of communication leads to permanent human impoverishment in almost every field. Or, consider the range of human experience that is deepened, enlarged, and made more joyous or more insightful by virtue of understanding the arts. As far as social studies—history, sociology, anthropology, and the like—are concerned, no one is going to ask an adult when Luther pinned his theses on the cathedral door, or when Galileo was forced to recant his discovery that the earth moved around the sun. But if a person does not know such things, he cannot understand what it means to be a modern man rather than a medieval man.

Compared with many so-called relevant topics introduced ad hoc into the school, these subjects are enormously significant. They are

[5] *Ibid.*

not immediately exciting to the untutored because their full relevance can only be grasped after long initiation. If educating is what we have claimed it to be, the task of educators is to devise ways and means of initiating their pupils into these secrets as early as possible.

INTERESTS

What of the child's interests? There are several problems connected with the notion of interests as a guide to curriculum. The psychological fact that the pupil must be interested is not the same thing as saying that the child's immediate interests are the proper focus of teaching. Human beings can be interested in almost anything, however mean or bizarre. One Nazi doctor was interested in how long children would live when deprived of fats in their diet. Human beings are often interested in things that are unworthy of their attention, and, conversely, they are uninterested in and perhaps unaware of many things from which they would benefit. Educating is interesting students in things that will be to their advantage as human beings.

We have seen that one of the things in which children are interested is understanding. To educate and to teach mean to build on this primary fact, otherwise, the educator becomes merely an entertainer.

NEEDS

How about a needs curriculum? This would seem to be more substantial a basis for education than mere interests. What are *human* needs? Students obviously have biological needs, but these are not of direct interest to the educator. The meeting of those needs is, primarily, the job of other social institutions. As soon as we talk about "social needs" or "growth," we enter a more debatable realm.

To speak of any specific human needs is to presuppose some view of human nature. The educator, who is a convinced social Darwinian, for instance, will have an entirely different view of what students need than, say, a Marxist or Christian. This will be true of every claim except, perhaps, a few relating to biological necessities like food, air, and shelter. Even here, the claim that these necessities ought to be shared in some equitable way is not merely a fact of some science. It is a moral claim.

Today one might object that many social needs are obvious, such as the need for job training, for instance. But there are many needs in our society; some militant blacks, for instance, would say that there is a need for training in social militancy, not adaptation to a racist society.

The point is that the notion of *needs* is highly ambiguous. It does not, *by itself*, help the educator to organize his work. No doubt, in the broadest sense, any educational system that can justify itself before the bar of reason will have to serve something fundamental in human nature, and *needs* may stand for that something. I suggest that naming it in this way is not much help.

In conclusion, it must be pointed out that one typically human need is the *need to understand* or the *need to share meanings*. This would seem to be the need that *educating* in its essential meaning is directed toward. Moreover, meeting this need by cultivating the power to understand is a precondition for any large satisfaction of the wider range of human needs. Understanding is the *metier* of educating. If educators do not make this a prime objective, no other group in society is likely to do so.

ADJUSTMENT

Critics of modern education have focused frequently on the effects of making *adjustment* a curricular goal. The results, they claim, are mass conformity and mediocrity. This is not a philosophical issue, but it becomes philosophical if we ask what *adjustment* means. In an essay on "The Concept of Adjustment," C. J. B. Macmillan contends that there seems to be a "gross misunderstanding rooted in the concept of adjustment; educational theorists and their critics seem to talk past one another whenever the topic of personal or social adjustment enters the discussion."[6]

[6] C. J. B. Macmillan, "The Concept of Adjustment," in Komisar and Macmillan (eds.), *Psychological Concepts in Education*, p. 60.

Adjustment in a psychological sense is any accommodation of the person to his environment. Even if the child becomes a truant, says Macmillan, he has in this sense *adjusted* to his environment by running away from it. For the purposes of education, it is necessary to add something to the purely descriptive meaning of the term. Whether consciously or not, the educator means by *adjustment* some *proper* relationship to other people and the environment. *Proper*, however, introduces a norm not immediately derivable from the psychological descriptions. To be sure of the meaning of *proper*, it is necessary to have some standards or criteria of that which is adequate or *good* human behavior.

Running away is thought to be an improper response to the educational environment. The withdrawn student has also adapted, but in a way that the educator views as unsatisfactory. If we look at it from the teacher's point of view, we can ask whether, say, drugging the student should count as a *teaching* method. Many *overly active* students, we are told, are given drugs to quiet them so that they can conform to the classroom situation. Up to a point, this is innocent enough, but surely there comes a point where drugging a student so that he is passively submissive is contrary to the purpose of educating. Yet, from a purely descriptive point of view, this would count as *adjustment* of a sort.

Macmillan cites the discussion of adjustment in Laurence F. Shaffer and Edward J. Shoben's textbook, *The Psychology of Adjustment*, to show what psychologists mean by the concept. According to Shaffer and Shoben, life is a sequence of need arousal and need satisfaction. Behaviors are adjustive because "they reduce tensions."[7]

Macmillan argues that to substitute "reduce tensions" for "adjust" in the context of education is absurd. If you ask a teacher whether a given child is adjusting, the reply, "Yes, he is reducing his tensions," would be educationally unilluminating. Even to say that Johnny is adjusting in the sense of reducing the tensions aroused by the school routine would not help. As we have seen, running away would be one form of adjustment in this case. Thus, it would appear that the psychologist and the educationist mean different

[7] *Ibid.*, p. 65.

things by saying that "Johnny is adjusting to the school routine."[8]

The theory of tension reduction is too simplistic for educational purposes, failing to make distinctions that are educationally important, the distinctions, for instance, among the tensions of thwarting, of hunger, of intellectual attention, of anticipation, of joyful excitement, and so on. Distinctions like these, of great subtlety and variety, are common in ordinary language, as Austin and other analysts have pointed out. This is why it is possible to use the ordinary language analysis of analytic methods to criticize technical proposals when they are applied to a wider range of phenomena than is warranted.

Ambiguities of this kind in the concept of *adjustment* compelled Macmillan to conclude that psychological theory is "inadequate for use in theories designed to guide educational practice."[9]

LEARNING TO LEARN
AND LEARNING TO THINK

Criticisms of curricula based upon retention of information are congenial to the claims we have made for the meaning of both teaching and educating. These critics say that the schools should make a much larger place in the curriculum for what might be called cognitive competencies as distinguished from cognitive retention. What counts in education, they say, is not the information one can remember, but the skills one has attained in learning and thinking. There are other competencies that belong to the same family of related concepts: learning to solve problems, to inquire, to discover, to think critically, and to create. If we are to understand what is proposed when it is recommended that students' *learn to learn* or *learn to think*, and so on, there are some conceptual ambiguities to be clarified.

(1) Learning to learn is learning an activity not a sum of knowledge. It is learning *how* to do something. In this sense, we may think of it as a skill. It is a kind of competence in doing, like swimming or playing the piano.

[8] *Ibid.*, p. 68.
[9] *Ibid.*, p. 61.

(2) It is different from learning the skill involved in swimming. Learning to swim is to learn to do one thing, whereas learning to learn is becoming competent in a whole *class* of activities. Human beings can learn to perform an enormous range of activities from doing science or meditating, to horseback riding, or karate. What needs to be clarified is whether there is a single body of instruction that can make learning all these things easier.

When Dewey proposed his five steps of thought, he believed that he had exposed the natural structure of being intelligent in the world. When we say someone is "intelligent," we mean that he can learn something quickly. Dewey thought intelligence was a biological notion derived from the survival pattern of the race, and these five steps were a clarification of that basic pattern. He also thought science was the model of intelligent activity, and the five steps were a commonsense version of all scientific reflection. Dr. J. Richard Suchman and his group at the University of Illinois have followed Dewey in their studies of "inquiry training." They have elaborated these steps of thought into a teaching technique they claim can bring a student to a high level of competence in *problem solving* or *inquiry*. The technique consists in putting the student into a situation where a concrete problem serves as a focal point of his investigation. The adult environment must be responsive to the child's efforts without giving him ready-made answers. The teacher must make additional information available as the student requires and offer sequences of goals or plans of action, but he must not infringe upon the student's own territory by taking over the direction of his thought. Suchman claims statistical proof that this method works well.

Perhaps it does, but this does not answer the question that we have raised: Is there a universal technique of intelligence? It is not sufficient to show that some techniques are capable of generality, or that the methods in some of the sciences are applicable to many commonsense situations. As valuable as this is, it does not establish that the person who masters such a technique has really *learned to learn*. He may have learned a technique that is more general than the activity of learning one type of material, but he would still fall short of having mastered the key to universal intelligence.

There are other dimensions of understanding that are not covered by such a pattern. The pattern of thought we are using in this book, conceptual analysis, for instance, does not follow these five steps, nor does it illuminate, without serious amendment, what it means to learn about values or to think in moral, aesthetic, or religious categories.

There are more serious objections to thinking of learning to learn or to think as a technique. We discussed these reasons when we searched for behavioral equivalents to thought. We learned in that discussion that there is simply no limit to the moves that intelligence makes in inventing and creating. This does not mean that there is no value in formulating strategies that have been widely useful in certain types of problems, but it is a chimera of the technician that all these moves can be spelled out. There is, furthermore, a contradiction in the desire to find a universal technique and the claim of the educational critics that contemporary education ignores the intelligence and autonomy of the student. In its final meaning, this proposal for teaching everyone a universal technique is like the very programming of the student that is so offensive to these educators.

Let us turn from this general question to a few specific ones. When it is proposed that students *learn to learn*, it is not clear just what is meant. Here are some possibilities: (1) It could mean this mastery of a universal technique; (2) it could mean simply that the student be disposed to keep on learning after he leaves school; or (3) it could mean a generalize capacity to understand.

There is a real difference between (1) learning to learn, and (2) learning to be a learner. Learning to be a learner, which is, I think, nearer to what educators who follow this line really seek, is significantly different from learning to learn. It would be perfectly sensible to say, "He 'learned to learn' in school, but he has done precious little learning since." Learning to *be* something is not the same thing as learning to *master* something. The latter includes, among other things, a discrimination among values and a decision with regard to them that leads to a disposition to be one kind of person rather than another. There is no reason to suppose that, say, *learning to swim* is the same as *deciding to be a swimmer*. Something like the later statement appears to be what is involved in the proposal *learning to learn*.

There is also a difference between the mastery of a general technique and a generalized capacity to understand. Consider the differences among the following:

(1) Learning to "parrot" chemical formulae.[10]
(2) Learning to do chemistry—the ability to perform chemical experiments, and so on.
(3) Learning the logos of chemistry—learning not only to do chemistry, but to know what one is doing when he is experimenting, hypothecating, and so on.
(4) Learning to perform in other fields of knowledge as well as chemistry.
(5) Learning the logos of these other fields.
(6) Learning the interrelationships of the logos of these fields to one another.

The last item would require a grasp of the wide variety of human modes of understanding. This would be what I have called the real meaning of *educating*, namely, to become initiated into the realms of human meaning.

One of the advantages of this last concept of *learning to learn* is that the sheer awareness of such a range of human meanings that comes about in a genuinely liberal education carries with it dispositional features. That is, there is a high likelihood, if not the certainty, that a person educated in this way will retain a taste for understanding after he has left formal schooling behind.

CREATIVITY AND CRITICISM

Before we leave this topic we should look at a couple of other items that illustrate conceptual analysis in education. The first is to ask what *creativity* means. Tests on *creativity*, for example, often include questions that explore the student's ability to think unconventionally about certain topics. One test asks the student to "Write down as many unusual uses as possible for a brick."[11] The criterion

[10] The phrase "learning to parrot" is used by Alburey Castell in "Pedagogy Follows Learning Theory," in Komisar and Macmillan (eds.), *Psychological Concepts in Education*, pp. 158–166.
[11] Gribble, *Introduction to Philosophy of Education*, p. 97.

of creativity in this question is the largest number of such "unusual uses." Does this test creativity?

Creativity certainly involves breaking away from conventional patterns, but by itself it may mean madness as well as genius. In addition to *novelty*, creativity involves at least three other criteria. The unconventionally bizarre or crazy is not in itself a mark of creativity. Only if the new production has a more complex rationale and significance than what preceded it can it count as an instance of creativity. A new vase, a mechanical invention, or a new theory must not only be different, but it must possess a fresh beauty or usefulness. What is merely nonconformist in thought or action, the merely unusual, cannot count as creativity. What is also missing in the identification of creativity with mere unconventionality is the failure to recognize the high level of discipline manifested by inventors, poets, and painters. Their discipline includes not only the struggle for a personal technique suited to their talents, but also a rich background of knowledge in the art or science in which they are working.

There is, to be sure, a logos of creativity in the broad sense. Good descriptions of the "creative process" are available from such scholars as Brewster Ghiselin.[12] This logos, however, does not include precise techniques for guaranteeing creativity itself. What a person can learn from such descriptions are some general truths about people who have been creative in various fields, but there are no guarantees that one will become a poet, painter, or scientific discoverer.

Another concept that appears in many curriculum proposals is *learning to be critical*. If we think of this in terms of techniques, we might imagine that drilling students in stock critical moves would make them into good critics or develop their powers of critical thinking. John Passmore argues that this would be merely a form of indoctrination. Cleverness in analysis is not the same thing as being a good critic. " 'Being critical'," Passmore writes, "is, indeed, more like the sort of thing we call a 'character trait' than it is like a skill. To call a person 'critical' is to characterize him, to describe his nature, in a sense in which to describe him, simply, as

[12] Brewster Ghiselin (ed.), *The Creative Process* (New York: New American Library, 1955).

'capable of analysing certain kinds of fallacy' is not to describe his nature."[13]

To learn to be critical is then dispositional as much as technical. To learn this depends much more on the attitude and example of the teacher and the atmosphere of the school than upon any concrete techniques. If the teacher thinks that *being critical* means merely finding fault with everything that confronts him, he will not set an example of the critical spirit. He may produce a crop of mere faultfinders. In order to develop criticism in the best sense, writes Passmore, "a teacher has to develop in his pupils an enthusiasm for the give-and-take of critical discussion."[14] The key element is the revelation to the student that the teacher himself can be wrong, that his authority is not infallible. Where this happens the teacher has an opportunity to demonstrate the critical spirit by revising what he has taught. He thus demonstrates in rational discussion that it is evidence and reason that count, not persons.

CONFLUENT EDUCATION

The term "confluent education" is used by educators who propose that the curriculum should include affective as well as cognitive elements. They are more concerned with attitudes, values, personal awareness, and interpersonal relations than with knowledge. In life, they say, these things are never separated, and if education is for living, then it would seem plausible that they should be joined there as well.

Here several analytical issues are raised. What, for instance, are the similarities and differences among (1) coming to know, (2) coming to value, and (3) coming to be. In an essay entitled "Coming to Value and Getting to Know," Alburey Castell contrasts these two activities.[15] To say, "I know X" is to say something quite different from "I value X." To be sure, he points out, if a person did

[13] John Passmore, "On Teaching To Be Critical," in R. S. Peters (ed.), *The Concept of Education*, p. 195.

[14] *Ibid.*, p. 198.

[15] Remarks on a paper, "Value Conflict," by Harry S. Broudy, presented at a conference at the University of Oklahoma in November, 1963.

not value some things like consistency, clarity, verifiability, and even knowing, he would not get to know anything. On the other hand, you cannot value something you do not know about. Thus, these two activities—knowing and valuing—are related, but different. In Castell's view, educators should realize that their real concern is with *coming to know*, that is, with what he calls "liquidating ignorance" rather than with valuing. He contends that trying to get someone to value something, except in the indirect sense mentioned above, cannot count as *teaching*. I think that this may be only partially correct.

The issue seems to me to lie in the question whether there is a logos of valuing as there is logos of knowing. I believe that there is. I will discuss this at some length in the next chapter, but here it will be enough to appeal to the *Taxonomy of Educational Objectives* previously cited. Volume II of *Taxonomy* examines so-called "affective learning." The authors describes this process as follows: (1) There is first the receiving or attending to certain value experiences. (2) Then, some kind of response to the phenomenon in question and finding satisfaction in the response follows. (3) At the third stage, the items of evaluation begin to take on some consistency and stability. At this stage, the student notes his own preferences and makes tentative personal commitments. (4) Gradually, these evaluations evolve into a *system of values* through increased conceptualization, emerging in stage (5) as a characterization of personality of the learner. The value complexes become more or less permanently a part of his unique value-attitude system. At this last stage, the individual has integrated these beliefs, ideas, and attitudes into a single philosophy or world view that is his own.

A glance at the taxonomy of cognitive learning reported earlier will show how many striking parallels there are between the two types of learning. This *Taxonomy* supports rather substantially the view that there is a rationale to learning values. Where there is a rationale there can be *teaching*.

To be sure, valuing is not something that can be grasped as a pure concept; it remains to the very last a type of data. This is also true in scientific knowing. In science, the data are not reduced to concepts, but their relationships are structured conceptually. When I know something scientifically, my knowing is never identical with the thing known, which remains a datum of my experience, but I am said to know it when the relationship of this sensory datum to other data is made clear through thought.

In this sense, I agree with Castell, teaching about valuing is not the same thing as inducing a specific kind of valuing in the student. However, it is so significantly close to the process by which valuing is changed and enriched that the closeness should be acknowledged.

LEARNING TO BE

The same can be said of the concept *learning to be*, the search for character, personal identity, or self-knowledge. *Human becoming* has a rationale that has been recently elaborated in the work of psychologists, such as Erick Erickson, Carl Rogers, and the late Abraham Maslow, who have directed their research toward what they call "human potentialities." Like the cognitively oriented educators who decline to consider personal becoming as legitimate curriculum, these psychologists tend to despise cognitive learning. Rogers writes, "Anything that can be taught to another is relatively inconsequential, and has little or no significant influence on his behavior."[16] He says that he has "lost interest in being a teacher," and that the outcomes of teaching "are either unimportant or hurtful." Insofar as he is underscoring the need for interest and participation in learning on the part of the learner, he is undoubtedly right. The tenor of his proposals is to limit education to the kind of thing he has found important in psychotherapy, namely, the process of *coming to be* rather than *coming to know*. I have already indicated why I think this is an insufficient account of education.

The proposal that these writers are offering to educators—to make education more affectively significant—is worth examining. The proposal as an educational matter hinges on the presence of a genuine rationale in the process of becoming, a rationale that can be taught. The schools are not the only institutions charged with helping human beings become more human by fulfilling their per-

[16] Carl Rogers, *On Becoming a Person* (Boston: Houghton Mifflin, 1961), p. 275.

sonal potentialities. This has been the traditional role of the family and the church. Lately, it has been taken over by the psychotherapeutic branches of medicine.

The question is this: What is the peculiar role of education in this matter? My reply is that the educator's primary role is with the *rationale* of personal growth, with the *understanding* of these personal processes that go on both in and out of institutions. Whatever has a rationale can be taught. Erickson, for instance, has elaborated the stages in human becoming from infancy to maturity. The rationale of that process is surely as important as the study of mathematics or history. Of course, the wise teacher knows that this rationale cannot be understood unless he refers to the present experience of the student as a kind of laboratory in which these concepts are tested and made comprehensible.

HABITS

Let me close this discussion with a consideration of a term commonly used in connection with *character* education. I refer to the concept of *habit*. It is sometimes said that the teacher should inculcate good habits in his students. Some educators are of the opinion that an educated person is one who has learned a set of useful habits, especially, in Dewey's phrase, "the habit of intelligence."

I doubt that this language is felicitous. In fact, the expression "habit of intelligence" seems to be a contradiction in terms. When we speak of a person having a habit of biting his nails or smoking cigarettes, we suggest not only something bad that he does, but also that the compulsion to do so is also bad. A habit is an activity that goes on without, or even in spite of, thought. Nor does it make much sense to cure bad habits by counter habits. A compulsion not to bite one's nails or a compulsion not to smoke would not necessarily be good. Nonsmoking is not the same as having a habit of not smoking.

A habit is a pattern of behavior that is set off automatically by a set of stimuli. It, like the notion of conditioning, suggests automaticity, and is chiefly appropriate to bodily processes or activities. No doubt, automatic reactions can be useful under certain conditions, such as battlefield behavior or participation in a sport. The range of application of the notion of *habit* to education lies in this region of *training*. It does not make sense to speak of the "habit of honesty" or the "habit of thinking independently."

There are several reasons for this. The first is that being honest, for instance, is a norm controlled activity, in the sense that the actor behaves in certain ways *because* of certain norms. Honesty cannot be a simple reflex. To be honest means to know the meaning of such complex notions as *ownership, property, rights,* and so on, plus a set of principles that are applicable to a wide variety of situations. To be honest is not a reflex conditioned to fixed situations. It can be applied in new situations which one has never before encountered.

What has been said of honesty applies even more emphatically to the quality of being intelligent. Being thoughtful or honest are dispositions to behave in accordance with complex norms, not habits of reflexive behavior in the presence of stimuli patterns. Given the stimuli, we can predict the behavior in the case of a habit, but this is not true of the behavior of an honest man. To be sure, there are things that can be predicted of an honest man; he will not steal in situations where theft is clearly defined. His positive acts are not predictable in this way. The honest thing to do in a complex situation cannot be predicted, it must be thought out in accordance with the notions of integrity of the actor himself. Of course, he may make a mistake that he will regret. Habitual behavior cannot be mistaken. One may have a bad habit, but the habit cannot be mistaken. In the case of a disposition to behave in honest ways, a person may regret that he did not apply his norms accurately. What the educator is concerned with is not habits but dispositions, and dispositions include that ingredient of understanding that belongs to education.

WHAT IS A SCHOOL?

This question is philosophically awkward because it is partly historical and partly analytical. What we are seeking is the distinctive role of the school in society. In primitive societies, we do not find that division into specialized institutions and agencies that characterize our own. Though, to some extent, there is much overlapping of function, each of the major institutions of society—the state, family, business, church, and school—performs characteristic services unique to that institution. A modern society is impossible without schools for the simple reason that the degree of education required of its citizens is both too broad and too specialized to be left to other social institutions. This is its sociological rationale.

The school is the place of *teaching* and *educating, par excellence.* It is the place for systematically cultivating the human capacity to understand. Take this away and the school's unique significance disappears. The school is a repository of past knowledge, the center for new inquiry, and the medium for initiating successive generations in the secrets of learning.

Society acts through the school to preserve and perpetuate itself. The school is one of the major links between generations, one of the agencies for initiation of the young into the ongoing society. If the society is dynamic like our own, rather than traditional, then this act of self-preservation cannot be one of merely coming to terms with things as they are. Society will inevitably have to prepare the individual to participate in the movement of society toward its own possible futures. This fact makes the debate over adjustment versus transformation somewhat *academic* in the bad sense. Whenever the student is adjusted to a moving stream, he is bound to need the skills and knowledge for moving wisely with society's preponderant currents of change.

The direction of these currents is not fixed or predetermined. A society has many potential futures at a given time. Educators cannot avoid making some decisions about which of those possibilities are to be actualized. For better or worse, educators have to direct their energies toward the things most worth knowing as a society's potentiality moves toward its actualization, that is, the information, skills, attitudes, and values that belong to the future desired by the members of that society.

When, for instance, we consider education in a democracy, we need at least some reasonably clarified notion of what defines a *democratic* state of affairs, and, to put it behaviorally, what concrete styles of life contribute to that social ideal. There is bound to be tension between the school and certain segments of the community. In racial matters, for instance, the schools of a democracy have no choice but to arrange some amicable, equal, and just relationship among the races, if they are to be faithful to the democratic proposition. Nor can they remain content with a nineteenth-century class notion of what constitutes American education.

Aside from the question of how to best prepare the young to contribute to the continuity of American society, there is another claim: the individual himself. It is not enough to look at him entirely from the social point of view. He has a right to expect that his schooling will endow him with some of the means for becoming a full human being. The happy coincidence of social needs and personal fulfillment is a consummation devoutly to be wished, but, as Freud observed, civilizations have a way of bequeathing a certain amount of discontent to its citizens. This tension between personal growth and social usefulness is bound to last as far as we can foresee, and it must be taken into account by the schools. Generations of human potential may not be sacrificed lightly to social expediency by any society that calls itself good, especially by a democracy that presumably exists for the welfare of its members. Thus, we have three themes that must be constantly woven into the composition of education: the present and the future needs of society and the potentialities of individuals.

Much of what we have said applies not only to schools, but to governments, churches, and indeed to all institutions. What may then be said of the school specifically? We can answer this by combining what has been said about the school's specialized function and meaning with the above observations about the needs of society and the individual. The school as society's institutionalization of understanding discharges its obligation to both the society and the individual by initiating its students into the rationale of the major realms of human meaning. In so far as such an understanding prepares the individual for his place in society, both present society and that of the future, and enables him to develop as an authentic person, the school has discharged its proper function.

All this does not mean that schools may not perform some noneducational tasks. It does mean that the central focus of its function and meaning should be perfectly clear. Otherwise, as we have seen in so many communities, the schools are burdened with all sorts of noneducational activities from baby-sitting to public entertainment. Communities are often tempted to burden the schools in this way because the schools have the children in custody for so many hours of the day. We have already seen that this captivity is one of the liabilities of compulsory education, and to use it to further dilute the process is educationally debilitating.

WHAT IS A UNIVERSITY?

The meaning of education is more visible at the upper end of the process than at the beginning. This is not surprising. The seed is more manifest in the flower and fruit than in its early shoots. With the current ferment in higher education, it might be useful to see if there is some unique meaning to the notion of a university.

Suppose that colleges and universities were abolished and all their functions were parcelled out to other institutions. Would anything be lost? Let social clubs and marriage bureaus arrange the marriages that are now formed during college years. Let training for trades and professions be carried forward in institutes attached to the appropriate industries. Let the present tendency of the young to make a religion out of education be redirected to the churches. Citizenship training and related attitude formation could be parcelled out to informal community programs, television, and the press. Perhaps hardest of all, let athletic clubs take over the public entertainment aspect of intercollegiate athletics. What would be missing if the college and university were thus to disappear?

What would be missing would be any center where learning is enjoyed for its own distinctive worth, a setting in which the unfolding of the understanding is prized for itself. There would be no place that systematically cultivated the broad range of human meanings that have become the funded and growing treasure of civilized existence.

What are some of the presuppositions of such an educational center when it is functioning in accordance with its historic though unwritten charter? The first is freedom. Freedom is a *sine qua non* for genuine inquiry that pursues the meaning of any subject matter without prejudice. Where the conclusion is foregone, the inquiry is precluded. It is also a necessary ingredient in the educational ideal of putting the student in complete possession of all his powers. He must be free to experiment with his own values and concepts, and to discover what the civilized tradition means to him. This is the basic rationale of the much debated tenure of professors and academic freedom. To the public tenure is often viewed as a guaranteed job or sinecure, but its real meaning lies in the effort to put the teacher beyond threats to his freedom to teach and to inquire, following, as Socrates said, the argument where it leads. It has no other justification.

A second presupposition of higher education is respect for persons. Kant, in his second formulation of the famous categorical imperative, said that a rational man may never treat another person merely as a means, but always as an end in himself. He deduced this rule from his first formulation of the same imperative, namely, that a rational man will always universalize his actions, never making himself an exception. The logical connection here is simple: The man who appeals to reason appeals to it equally in every other man and must respect that other man as an agent of reason. No doubt, there are other grounds for respecting people, and one of them is connected intimately with the educational task: Without a high degree of mutual respect, genuine learning cannot go on.

A third presupposition of higher education is respect for truth itself as it unfolds to human inquiry. Truth, like justice, is no respecter of persons. In the presence of truth there is no appropriate response but acceptance, with only such reservations as are presupposed in the necessity for further inquiry. Moreover, truth has a universal element. It is no more a respecter of nations or cultures or races than it is of individuals. The university is thus a transnational global institution. It stands for an ideal that judges the claims of all special groups and cultures.

A further presupposition of higher education is the unity of knowledge. This unity is not a present possession but an ideal. The quest of understanding presupposes the eventual ideal unity of the realms of meaning. The compartmentalization of knowledge into disciplines and sciences may be a convenience, but the university must protect itself against the fragmentation that such compartmentalization fosters. The learner is a single mind with the desire to see things in their togetherness, not mere ad hoc togetherness, but meaningful togetherness. This is hard to hold in focus in a world where knowledge explodes in so many directions. It was easier in the medieval university where this unity, according to John Henry Newman, "was realized and acted on . . . with a distinctness unknown before; all subjects of knowledge were viewed as parts of one vast system, each with its own place in it, and from knowing one, another was inferred."[17] In the modern university there is no such single system, but there cannot be a university in the real sense that does not presuppose such a unity and that does not search diligently for it.

What of the current drive to turn the university into an active force for social change? Several factors have conspired to bring this about. One is the rising generation's tendency to make higher education into a kind of religious surrogate: a center of social ideals and repository of the means for achieving full personhood. This is not too surprising in the light of declining public enthusiasm for official religion coupled with the ideal notion of the university that I have just outlined. Another factor is the increasing criticism of modern society and the desire to see it changed without delay. When we consider that university is the first institution that young people encounter as they emerge into adulthood, it is natural that they should see it as the ready instrument for carrying out their hopes for the world and for themselves.

We have seen that education in a dynamic society is as inevitably committed to the future as to the past, and that social change is bound to be in part a by-product of the way educational decisions are made. However, it is another matter to turn the university into a political agency for direct social action. Even enlightened political action is inevitably partisan, and no matter how urgent it may be at the time, it is no substitute for the work of detached critical analysis that marks the unique task of a university. Moreover, the uni-

[17] Dwight A. Culler, *The Imperial Intellect* (New Haven: Yale University Press, 1955), p. 188.

versity's commitment to learning for its own sake can be perverted by making it a mere means to any end no matter how good the end may be.

Students are no doubt right in demanding a larger share in the decisions that must be made in university life, but there is a limit to what can be done within the confines of a university without perverting its essential charter. When students and faculty abandon their work as students of society and turn to political action, they leave the school behind and put their faith in a political institution rather than education. If they turn the university into a partisan enterprise, they will, to this extent, destroy it as a place of learning.

To be sure, involvement in affairs is one good way to motivate learning. If students and teachers remain in a neutral vacuum regarding the urgencies of society, learning will diminish accordingly. This is only to say that social involvement at the university serves fundamentally the purpose of stimulating learning. From the university's point of view, social change and even personal growth are happy by-products of growth in understanding. When the formula is turned around, the university as a unique institution disappears. To see this with great clarity, we have only to see the fate of the political universities of Germany and Russia under Hitler and Stalin.

As a recent Harvard report put it: "The university—any university —has a distinctive competence, a special nature. That competence is *not* to serve as a government, or a consulting firm, or a polity, or a pressure groups, or a family, or a kind of secularized church; it *is* to serve as a center of learning and free inquiry."[18]

We are presented with a paradox that must be accepted if university education is to survive. The paradox is this: Higher education can serve society best by being itself, that is, a place of learning and understanding. That its learning should be relevant to the urgencies of personal and social life goes without saying. If it turns into a practical program for self-growth or social change, it will lose its distinct reason for being. Unfettered learning is a great social solvent. No social program founded on untenable ideals or the distortion of facts can long endure the light of critical examination. For

[18] *The University and the City* (Cambridge: The Office of the President, Harvard University, 1969), p. 6.

the same reason, a regimen of personal development that is unable to withstand the light of reason cannot survive.

What I have been saying is that the university is a unique institution with its own charter of existence. Humanity has a high stake in letting the university be the university.

All of this has a bearing on the lower schools as well. The ultimate significance of education at the lower levels is eventually to come to fruition in the kind of thing that a university represents. To be sure, many students will not extend their formal education beyond high school, but, insofar as possible, they should be initiated into the ideals of education for which the university stands.

10

VALUES

An initial difficulty awaits the analytic philosopher who raises the question of values in education. The opinion prevails, not without reason, that critical philosophy tends more to undermine values than to establish them. This opinion finds support in the history of empiricism from Hume to the present. As we saw in the first chapter, the immediate predecessor of ordinary language analysis was logical-empiricism, a view that received popular expression in Ayer's *Language Truth and Logic*. There Ayer relegated value statements, along with metaphysical and religious talk, to the region of subjective feeling. Such a view is not auspicious for anyone looking for guidance in sorting out their values, for it says in effect that there is no rationale whatsoever to valuing unless it be

146

sociological or psychoanalytic. As Jawaharlal Nehru once said, "I am strongly attracted to an ethical view of life, but I would find it hard to justify logically." In this opinion, he mirrors the views of empirical philosophers like Bertrand Russell. Yet these men would have undoubtedly agreed that no issue is more urgent in present society and education than the status of morality and values.

No major decisions about education can be made without some judgment about what ought to be done. Educators are challenged from the left and right, by the poor, by the blacks and other minorities, and by the young themselves. Traditional values no longer seem adequate and no criteria for making new choices seem compelling. This educational perplexity is a mirror of our bewildered society struggling through a period of serious threats to its very existence.

If, in a day of such conflicting counsel, philosophy can speak only of and about the sciences, but can say nothing to this perplexity, its usefulness to educators is, to say the least, pitifully limited. In this chapter, I hope to show that recent developments in the analytic tradition are not only congenial to value discussions, but that they have begun to illuminate the rational search for valid criteria. I do not want to exaggerate this claim, nor to suggest anything final about it. Warnock, in his book on *Contemporary Moral Philosophy*, concludes by saying that "This is a subject in which there is still almost everything to be done."[1] Analysis is in a phase of serious investigation of moral questions and the upshot is more a matter of intelligent conjecture than rational assurance. The conjecture is based upon a prediction that as moral language is subjected to clarifying analysis a new respect will be gained for the inherent rationality of evaluation and practical decision making.

VALUE PRESUPPOSITIONS IN EDUCATION

Every human activity presupposes values that are essential to that activity. Science, for instance, presupposes the worth of knowing those things that science discovers. If you deny the proposition

---

[1] G. J. Warnock, *Contemporary Moral Philosophy* (New York: St. Martin's Press, 1967), p. 77.

that these things are worth knowing, there would be no sense in doing scientific work. Similarly, education presupposes certain principles and values that must be accepted if one is to take education seriously. These principles and values fall into two groups: Those that are inherent to discussion about the school and its curriculum, and those that are inherent to teaching and learning.

Establishing schools, for instance, presupposes that education is doing some kind of good to somebody, benefitting both the young and the society as a whole. Whatever our rationale for these values, this kind of activity makes no sense whatsoever without presupposing this benefit.

The school shares with all social agencies the presumption that their existence is justified by their human effects. They are shot through with value assumptions. The curriculum, in particular, presupposes that it is knowledge most worth having. This is true whether we are talking about skills, humane learning, or science.

This may seem obvious, but it is a very important observation. It follows that if there is no rational foundation to moral deliberations, comparable in some way to the rationale of our scientific deliberations, then the whole enterprise of deciding about social policies is vain, or at least arbitrary. If it is arbitrary, the only final arbiter must turn out to be sheer unprincipled force. In Plato's *Republic*, Thrasymachus argued in exactly this way. What men call "justice," he said, is simply the rule of the strong in their own interest. Socrates countered by pointing out that strong rulers, lacking some kind of principles about values, would not know their real interests and would, therefore, not know what rules to promulgate and enforce.

The point is that sheer power may enable men to enforce their own policies, but it does not illuminate what policies they would really prefer if they knew what was the best for them. Practical deliberation, in short, is impossible without presupposing some rational order of evaluation. Thrasymachus assumed that men already knew what they wanted, and that what they wanted was in their best interests. The history of personal or social decisions unilluminated by reason is a melancholy record of disillusion.

The second area in which education presupposes values is in the activity of teaching. Teaching, as we have come to view it, assumes that understanding itself is a value of high order. The philosopher John Stuart Mill asked: Which is better, Socrates unsatisfied or a fool satisfied? If we settle for the latter, there would be no reason to teach. Unless knowing is better than being ignorant, why teach? Mill thought that any man who had tasted knowledge and compared it with his former ignorance would naturally prefer to know. The value of understanding certifies itself. There are other values of this kind, truth, beauty, and friendship, for instance. When they are experienced and understood, they are prized above falsehood, ugliness, and loneliness. The fool, said Mill, cannot appreciate such an argument because he is ignorant.

There are other values presupposed in teaching beside the worth of knowing as such. For instance, without freedom there can be no teaching, and if freedom is not prized, teaching becomes impossible. Here are some others: mutual personal respect of teacher and learner, the value of intellectual or physical discipline, and the worth of the subject matter taught. The absence of any of these would preclude the activity of teaching. When, for instance, we teach a youngster to concentrate or to organize his ideas we teach him a value as well as a procedure: the value of a focused and ordered mind. When we teach him to analyse, we presuppose the value of criticism. Writing, speaking, and reading presuppose the value of communications with his fellows in the human community.

So much for the values inherent in the immediate circle of educational activities. Here larger questions remain to be considered. What about moral education? What personal and social values should be taught to the young beyond those inherent in educational activity as such? What rational justification can be given for decisions about such questions? This brings us to the larger question of moral philosophy.

A NEW MORAL PHILOSOPHY

In his essay entitled "Toward a Philosophy of Moral Education,"[2] Frankena notes that despite the interest of the recent past in

---

[2] William K. Frankena, "Toward a Philosophy of Moral Education," in Scheffler (ed.), *Philosophy and Education*, chapter 11.

"character education" and "moral spiritual values in education," no really significant philosophical work on moral education has appeared since the works of Dewey and Durkheim. Fortunately, a generation of analytic philosophers has arisen, of whom Frankena is one, who have ventured beyond the limitations of the earlier skepticism of logical positivism, men like Wisdom, Toulmin, Hampshire, Nowell-Smith, Baier, Aiken, Edwards, Melden, and Rawls. These writers, among many others, have tried to clarify the rationale of moral activity. Many of the arguments in this chapter depend upon their work.

Analytic literature on moral philosophy tends to consider separately two different, though related, questions. The first has to do with ethics, with what Baier calls "the moral point of view." The second has to do with values. The logical problems related to these two issues are somewhat different as we shall see.

THE MORAL POINT OF VIEW

Let us examine what is involved in taking a moral point of view. Moral questions arise when there is a conflict of interests among people. If I ask the moral question, "What should I do?" what I am asking for is valid rules that would settle interest disputes in a reasonable way. There are several things that characterize moral situations. There is first this conflict of interests between two or more people. Unless other people are involved decisions do not involve moral questions, though they may involve value questions. Alone on his island, Robinson Crusoe had value decisions to make, but he had no moral problems until Friday came onto the scene. Before Friday arrived, he had no need of principles to mediate claims between him and anyone else, but he still had to decide how he was going to spend his time—smoking, and drinking coconut beer, meditating like a monk, or cultivating new skills, and so on.

A second feature of moral situations is that judgments must be impersonal. If Crusoe decides to do something to or for his man Friday, it is a genuinely moral decision only if he can agree that Friday should do the same to him if their situations were reversed. If he said, "I have just made a moral decision to do X which is only in my interest, but contrary to Friday's interest," a third party could properly ask, "Would you approve of Friday's making the same kind of decision if your situations were reversed?" If he said, "No," then the proper rejoinder would be, "Then why call it a *moral* decision?"

A third characteristic of moral judgments is universality. Suppose we ask Crusoe, "If two other people in this same situation were to ask your advice on what ought to be done, would you advise one of them in your present situation to do to the other what you intend to do to Friday?" If he said "No," then we would know that he did not understand the meaning of giving moral advice. A *moral decision must be universal in its application*. That is, advice is not moral that advises differently in situations that are in all relevant particulars the same. It may not allow irrelevant differences among people or situations to affect such judgments. Skin color, for instance, is in most cases an irrelevant consideration. If color is pleaded as a reason for a given decision, it is required to show why the color makes some real difference.

Suppose we ask, "But why should I be moral?" Two answers have been suggested to this question. The first is that almost everyone appeals to morality on his own behalf whenever he feels that he has been cheated or dealt with unfairly. He makes his claim as a person in the court of human interests. Once he makes such a claim he has already submitted his interests to the adjudication of moral reflection. He cannot remain rational and ask for moral consideration only when *his* interests have been violated.

The second reason for being moral is suggested by Baier. He says, "We should be moral because being moral is following rules designed to overrule reasons of self-interest whenever it is in the interest of everyone alike that such rules should be generally followed."[3] Baier's argument is, of course, not a moral argument. Nor should it be, since our question is why we should consider moral arguments in the first place. Baier's appeal is to prudence, not morality. However strong this argument might be, in most cases, it is still possible to reject its conclusion in particular cases without contradiction.

---

[3] Kurt Baier, *The Moral Point of View* (New York: Random House, 1965), p. 155.

Suppose a person had good reason to believe that he could violate moral rules secretly in his own interest, while appearing to everyone to be abiding by those rules. He could then congratulate himself that the effect of his behavior will be exactly the same as if he had acted morally. If he could steal, for example, without anyone knowing of the theft, then he could benefit from his act without publicly approving of theft. However, he would have to believe that very few members of his society would follow his example, and if they did, he would have to condemn their behavior as immoral.

The only consideration that could prevent this type of evasion would be if he prized personal integrity above prudence. But the worth of personal integrity cannot be rationally established on the grounds we have considered thus far. This brings us to a further question, whether there is any rational way to establish ideals or priorities among values—among them the value of being moral for its own sake.

So far, then, we have seen that morality has its own rationale. Once the moral point of view is adopted, certain conclusions follow. The only reason given for adopting the moral point of view is one of prudence. Practically speaking, it is of course a very powerful consideration. In a society which sought out wrongdoers so efficiently that violations of moral rules were promptly punished, this prudential consideration could be a very persuasive one. This was essentially Hobbes' argument for a strong state.

It is time now to examine whether there are valid rational arguments in support of value preferences or ideals. There are good reasons of economy why this question should be avoided if possible. Formal ethical theory is limited to the logic of *sharing* in whatever human beings are interested. It does not attempt to prescribe that in which they ought to be interested. If you try to answer the latter question by saying they should be interested in values that, say, would accrue to the *welfare of human beings*, a great many difficult questions arise. Any such prescription would have to presuppose, among other things, some knowledge of the true nature of being human. It would have to say, for instance, that no human being ought to value the extermination of a race of human beings, that this interest is somehow contrary to the best possibilities of men. Now, this is not far from common sense when it is not under the pressures of war or oppression. Most of our moral expressions presuppose it. It, however, presupposes that there must be open to inquiry the possibility of giving some rationally defensible ideal description of what a human being ought to be, or what kind of values he would choose if he knew what he was doing.

What follows is nothing like a complete answer to this question, nor is there space to indicate the inquiries that are being made into this matter, but it suggests a start on the question.

IS MORALITY PURELY FORMAL?

We have seen that the "moral point of view" is a purely formal argument. Morality dictates impartiality, fairness, and universality in the sharing of things thought to be valuable, but it does not give any grounds for deciding which things should be shared in this way. Hare asks us to consider the case of a Nazi official at a Jewish extermination camp being asked, "Suppose you discovered that you are a Jew, would you still think what you are doing is right?"[4] If he answered, "Yes, I would still believe that Jews should be exterminated," then he would have fulfilled the demands of the moral point of view. He would have shown a willingness to be impartial, fair, and universal in his judgment by not making himself an exception. No doubt, very few Nazis would have made this reply, but the fact that it is theoretically possible shows that a purely formal theory of morality has a serious limitation.

Warnock complains of the present status of moral philosophy in this same vein. He asks whether there is not more to the moral point of view than purely formal considerations. In the preceding example, would we say in any ordinary sense that the Nazi official was taking a defensible *moral* position? Is there not, asks Warnock, in moral feeling a sense that somehow what is called for is something that could be called concern for the welfare of human beings in general?[5] This, according to him, is one of those areas yet to be adequately analysed.

[4] Hare, *Freedom and Reason*, pp. 171–178.
[5] Warnock, *Contemporary Moral Philosophy*, p. 67.

Another element in moral sensibility that is not adequately clarified by a purely formal theory of morality is the feeling of what Kant called "unconditioned" or "categorical" obligation. The question might be put as follows: Why does a reasonable man feel the *compulsion* of moral demands? Kant thought that reason alone compelled him. It is a moot question whether the power of a reasoned argument is the same as the categorical obligation of a moral command. Why, for instance, does a person feel very strongly about keeping his promises, so strongly, in fact, that if he intends to break them, he offers extensive reasons for doing so. Why is the burden of proof felt so strongly by the promise-breaker? A psychologist might argue that the compulsion is irrational, and he might be right. But in common speech, we certainly distinguish very clearly between the compulsions of the insane and the compunctions of the sane. Moral compunction would seem to be one aspect of mental health. This, too, is a feature of moral language yet to be adequately analyzed. The following discussion may help illuminate part of this question, though not decisively.

THE LOGIC OF VALUES

Let us see whether adequate reasons can be given for preferring one set of interests to another. In the first place, it is clear that *many disputes over values can be settled by empirical means.* That is, the rules of scientific evidence can be used to decide some moral questions. This is true in three classes of value disputes. (1) Where the value in dispute is a *means* to another value already agreed upon. If, for instance, there is a difference of opinion about the worth of a certain course of action (X) that is alleged to lead to an agreeable result (Y), it is often possible to decide empirically whether, in fact, this sort of action has in the past led to such results as Y and whether in the future it is likely to do so.

(2) Empirical methods are also frequently, if not always, decisive in settling disputes over the evaluation of a given situation. In a court trial over an alleged case of negligence, for instance, the court cannot decide whether this is in truth an instance of negligence until the facts have been fully explored. The defendant

believes that the relevant facts will show him not to be negligent. The prosecution has beliefs to the contrary. The argument is largely a search for the facts—an empirical matter. Of course, in such an argument nonempirical questions will be raised, such as points of law and even philosophical considerations, such as, "Is a person who has just had a heart attack *negligent* when his car then strikes another?" Given agreement on such matters, the judgment of negligence hinges on the facts themselves. This does not mean that every reasonable man would agree that, given the facts, it is without doubt a case of negligence, for *negligence* is not one of the empirical facts. Any person who disputed the judgment would no doubt search for other facts in support of his difference of opinion.

The point of these remarks is that differences in judgments of value are often not really disputes over values, but over facts, and since we have reliable methods for reaching public agreement on facts, many value disputes can be settled in this way.

One classic instance where an appeal to facts changed the legal and moral evaluation of a social practice is the Supreme Court decision in 1954, on racially "separate but equal" schooling. For sociological reasons, the court found that "separate" in practice always meant "unequal," even where comparable facilities and funding were present. The implication of laws opposed to race mixing in the schools, they held, automatically created a climate inimical to equal educational opportunity. This decision is still disputed, but the dispute has now largely shifted to factual considerations. In this arena, the chances of eventual public agreement are higher than where the dispute is over a difference in value judgments.

To repeat the logic of this argument: Two situations that are exactly alike in every relevant respect must be valued in the same way. Value is not one of the facts of the situation, but the facts of the situation are relevant to a decision about its value. In such cases, it is not correct to say that evaluations are purely subjective.

(3) The third area in which facts are sometimes useful in settling value disputes is when an empirical examination of means-values shows that their cost is greater than the end-value sought. It might be desirable, and even possible, to use means X to attain value Y,

but if X turns out in some way to cost more than Y is worth, then reasonable men will decide against X. The United States could have "won" the Vietnam war, for instance, by killing everyone in North Vietnam, but even supposing this did not lead to a larger war, the moral enormity of paying this price does not seem worth such a "victory." Or, to use a domestic example, we could no doubt reduce highway mortality to near zero if we enforced a ten mile per hour traffic speed with a death penalty. In this case the price of the means-value seems too high even though the end-value is highly desirable.

CONSISTENCY IN VALUING

Rationality can be also seen presiding over decisions about value in a second important way, namely, in the application of the rule of consistency. If you can show a reasonable man that his evaluations are inconsistent with one another, he usually will acknowledge that he must modify them in some way to overcome the criticism. The adult with the fourth martini in his hand lecturing the young on drug abuse is not presenting a very impressive argument. The logic of the situation is evident to the young if not to adults. To be consistent without giving up the martini, the argument would have to be changed from "don't use drugs" to "use my drug rather than yours."

If education is the cultivation of reason in the student so that he is more capable of understanding himself and his environment, then it would seem that exploring discrepancies like this in our private and public life is a plausible educational activity. Lynd's study of the typical American "Middletown" shows that there is plenty of grist for this mill. Here are a few of the value contradictions to which he calls attention: (1) Individualism is a prime value, and "survival of the fittest" is a law of nature that made Americans great. But, people ought to be charitable, helpful to one another, loyal to the group, and work for common purposes. (2) Democracy is the ultimate form of living together because all men are created free and equal. But, you cannot trust popular votes and some people are "more equal" than others. (3) The family is our basic and most sacred institution. But, business is our most important institution and other institutions must conform to its needs. (4) America is really a "Christian nation." But, a man must make as much money as possible, and religion should stay out of economics and politics. (5) America believes in progress. But, the old tried fundamentals are best. People who desire change are suspected of being the dupes of foreign radicals.[6]

Neither a society nor a person enjoys having such contradictions pointed out, but it is fatuous to suppose that a rationally cultivated mind can overlook such tasks. This philosophical consideration is supported by the sociological fact that societies tend in varying degrees to be *systems* of values articulated through its various institutions. If the tensions among its values is too great, the society itself is in peril.

RULES FOR DECISION AMONG VALUES

A third way in which rationality presides over the activity of valuing lies in the way in which certain rules have emerged from the practice of reflective evaluation. These rules have been a part of value studies since Bentham and have been elaborated by his successors. For instance, a fruitful or fertile value is better than a sterile one. Other things being equal, a reasonable man will always choose a value that leads on to other values over one that is sterile of future satisfactions. The classical virtues, such as temperance and rationality, are fruitful in this way. Another rule is that a durable value, one that lasts a long time, is preferable to a short-run value. For much the same reason, a more intense and/or extensive value is preferable to a tepid or a narrowly applicable one.

To be sure, these rules are not always easy to apply in practice, and they do not constitute (as Bentham thought) a simple calculus of values, but in general they are often relevant considerations in any value dispute. What I mean by saying that they cannot be put into a simple calculus is illustrated by the fact that there is, for instance, no rule for preferring intensity to duration.

[6] Robert S. Lynd, *Knowledge for What?* (Princeton, N.J.: Princeton University Press, 1939), pp. 60–62.

THE FINAL TEST OF IDEALS AND VALUES

It would be wrong to assume that if the preceding assertions about reason in evaluation were true, values could be established by straightforward arguments alone. There is no way to make a value conclusion the inevitable result of a logical argument. When we desire to "prove" to someone else that an ideal or a value is authentic or valid for him, we may make many of the foregoing moves and still fall short of a demonstration. The final decision will have to be made by the person himself when he "sees" that you are right.

Take, for instance, the effort to demonstrate that a given painting is beautiful. If the person you are persuading does not see that it is beautiful, there are a number of things you can do. You can talk about its design, its agreeable composition, its symbolic significance, and so on, but the painting must somehow "show" itself to the viewer, establish its own value in his eyes. In this case, arguments are a complex kind of showing, first from this angle, then from that, but the conclusion must be "seen."

In the same way, an ideal, such as a democratic society, incorruptible personal integrity, or the values of becoming a knowledgeable person, and so on, cannot be logically driven home to anyone. However, these ideals and values can be displayed so carefully and so fully compared with their alternatives that it is reasonable to believe that most men, given time and attention, would come to approve them.

THE LOGIC OF MAKING VALUE DECISIONS

Many of the foregoing observations about the role of reasons in moral and value judgment find their natural context in practical decision making. *Scientific* decisions are made by a happy combination of logic and sense observations. Such decisions have a high standing in our judgment because they tend toward public agreement. Can anything comparable be said about practical decision making? Before scientific logic was known and widely accepted, men made factual judgments that were as much disputed as present-day value judgments. Perhaps (we should recognize that it represents a kind of faith judgment), if we explored the area of the practical deliberation with the same dedication that we have brought to cognitive deliberation, we could bring about a more general agreement on major value choices. At the very least, we would be clearer about what is really at dispute. Coming to know and coming to value are not the same thing, but they have analogous structures.

This change in the focus of inquiry from the logic of values to the logic of practical decision (valuing) promises a possible solution to some of the logical puzzles of past discussions. Aristotle long ago insisted upon the distinction between theoretical reason oriented to *knowing something* and practical reason oriented to *deciding what to do* about something.

The difference is important. Aristotle searched for the highest good *(summum bonum)*, and in modern times, Moore explored the meaning of *good* itself, but this is to treat values as objects of theoretical reason. It is when we turn to practical reason, to the business of deciding and evaluating, that we discover the context in which values appear. *Value* in this context becomes a classification word for modes of valuing rather than a substantive noun for some *thing* in the world. To search for the properties of this alleged *thing* has not been as helpful as philosophers hoped. It turns out, as we have seen from the discussion of the *Taxonomy*, that there may be a logic to deciding, just as there is a logic to knowing. It is in this context of asking, "What must I do?" rather than asking "What can I know?" that the logic of evaluation is made most clear.

DECISION MAKING

Here is one analysis of what goes on in making a decision. Much of it is a development of Dewey's "Five Steps of Thought," and shows at once some of the parallels between knowing and deciding.

(1) The first stage in decision making is a problematic situation. If this is a *knowing* situation, as in a scientific puzzle, the pattern is a cognitive one. If it is *practical* situation, then it calls for moral

and value directives. It is *problematic* because there are no ready to hand solutions. The first thing to clarify is the problem itself. Why is it felt as a problem? What is unsatisfactory? What values are threatened or desired that are not present? Why are customary solutions unsatisfactory? Such clarification also needs analytic reasoning to resolve questions concerning the meaning of the concepts involved.

(2) The second stage requires two moves: a factual one and an evaluative one. We must answer such questions as these: (a) What needs to be known in order to solve the problem? How can I find out? What biases are at work in making these factual inquiries? How do things look from different perspectives? (b) What principles are relevant? Are they consistent with one another? Can we agree on them? What values are at stake? What kind of priority can we give to them? Are they consistent with one another? Are compromises possible?

(3) The third stage of decision consists in formulating possible solutions. Here a new set of questions is asked: How do the respective proposals satisfy the various interests that are at stake? Are they fair? Are there other solutions that would be more value inclusive and fairer? Other questions similar to those asked in stage two are also relevant: What are the likely *factual* consequences of each alternative? What ideals, principles, and values are at stake in each of the proposals? Who will be hurt and who helped by them? Lastly, what wider significance would such a solution have beyond the immediate context of the problem at hand?

(4) Finally, the decision itself. Decision is not like the conclusion of a formal argument. What would count as a reasonable decision follows from the deliberation, but it is not conclusive. Reasonable men might differ, but there is a range beyond which they would not differ. The conclusion does indeed follow from the argument; it is not just a whimsical addition to it. The reasons for this are apparent. First, the whole process is very complex and requires problematic arrangements of values, differences among relevant ideals, and orders of priority in principles. In the nature of the case, this kind of thing is not as neat as mathematics. Second, practical deliberation prophesies a probable future, not a

certain one. There is bound to be an element of risk in such a prophesy.

Thus, *deciding* is not the same as concluding. To conclude that such and such is a wise course is not the same as deciding to follow it.

Decision making, then, has a logos, a rationale that can be taught. Teaching this logos is not the same as passing judgment on particular issues, nor is it the same as deciding to act in particular ways.

With all its defects, it can be safely said that the habit of reflection on decision making is likely to lead, in the long run, to more satisfactory results than other alternatives available to us. Also, it is the one method that can hope to make the grounds for decisions publicly known and debated.

THE LOGIC OF LEARNING VALUES

So far in this chapter two things have been noted: First, education presupposes values. Second, value talk and decision making have a rationale that qualifies them as something that can be taught. These conclusions are somewhat novel in the setting of modern empiricism though they are gaining support from the current analyses of moral and value language. Henry David Aiken, urging the importance of this element in education writes that "the concept of knowledge has been so badly misanalysed and misconceived in our western philosophical tradition that it might almost be better to say that the business of the learner is more with feeling or volition or sensibility than with something called 'cognition'."[7] I agree with the sense of his remark, but it must be added that as long as *feeling* and *volition* are looked upon as merely arbitrary personal matters, devoid of any rationale, an emphasis upon them could be a way of embracing a simple irrationalism. The burden of this chapter so far has been to show that feeling and volition have a rationale even if it is not the rationale of scientific cognition.

[7] Henry David Aiken, "Analytical Philosophy and Educational Development," in George Barnett (ed.), *Philosophy and Educational Development* (Boston: Houghton Mifflin, 1966), pp. 18–19.

Only if this is the case can we talk about *teaching* evaluation. I contend that value sensibility is not essentially more subjective than cognitive learning. Nicholas Rescher, in his *Introduction to Value Theory*, shows some interesting parallels:[8]

Cognitive	Evaluative
Belief	Valuing or desire
Correctness of belief	Correctness of valuing or desire
Believes to be true	Valued or desired
Actually true	Valuable or desirable

One thing noteworthy about this chart is that the concepts of *valuable* and *desirable* are not the same as simply *desired*. There may be such a thing as wrong desire just as there is such a thing as incorrect belief. Some thinkers go astray at this point by repeating Mill's famous fallacy of equating *desirable* with *being desired*. There is no contradiction in saying that you desire something undesirable. Or, conversely, you may not desire to learn, for instance, but it may be desirable that you do so. Authentic values, then, are in part the fruit of reflection.

A final critical word. Both Rescher and Bloom assume an atomic beginning to value learning, leading to more wholistic appreciation at a later stage. However, there is a counterhypothesis that should also be explored, the hypothesis that no value is ever noticed or acted on that does not *at the very first* belong, in some dim way at least, to one's overall perception of life—his *implicit* "philosophy of life." I suspect that value learning goes both ways. The child inherits culturally some perspective on life from his earliest years. He brings this to school with him. He may change this perspective as he learns, but it remains as an active element in his learning experience. This is the reason why a ghetto child, for example, often finds the values of middle-class society difficult to understand or even boring and uninteresting. His world is different even at the age of six. The teacher who wants to break through this barrier must understand the world-orientation of his pupil, and present values to him that make some sense in terms of his implicit world view.

[8] Nicholas Rescher, *Introduction to Value Theory* (Englewood Cliffs, N.J.: Prentice-Hall, 1969), p. 131.

What I am saying is that the learning of evaluation may move from whole to part just as much as from part to whole.

This counterhypothesis does not impair the conclusion we have already reached, namely, that there is a rationale in value-learning. Whether it is from part to whole or from whole to part, or both together, the same conclusion follows: Learning to value is not a random affair, it has a rationale of its own, a rationale that places it within the proper sphere of learning as an activity of understanding.

ARE MORAL CHOICES AND DECISIONS ABOUT VALUES RELATIVE?

The person who expects philosophical analysis to offer a logic of moral judgment and evaluation that leads to certainty and a set of absolutes will feel disappointed at the tentativeness of our conclusion. We have, indeed, arrived at a kind of relativism. Is such a conclusion of value to educators? I believe it is.

This relativism is not the same as scepticism. It does not say that one choice is as good as another or that some values are not better than others. Within limits, there are the kinds of choices reasonable men would make. Moreover, the longing for an absolutism that haunts this inquiry is, after all, a will-o'-the-wisp. In the past, there have been, to be sure, systems of absolute rules and value prescriptions. In practice, however, two things have occurred. Either these absolutes were amended to allow exceptions, or they were simply ignored. The commandment against killing, for instance, was amended to exclude criminals or foreign enemies. Killing in self-defense, for instance, was allowed, and so on.

Perhaps more practically, there is no set of absolutes that may be used as the basis of instruction in public schools. If such a doctrinaire ethic were offered simply as a set of divine imperatives without rational content, then they could not, on our premises, even be *taught*, they would have to be indoctrinated. The law furthermore prohibits the domination of the public school curriculum by any dogmatically guaranteed moral teaching. In any case, the great majority of today's citizens simply will not accept any such dogmatic moral code. Even those who remain faithful to the churches in which these codes had their origins are asking for reasons.

Finally, it can be pointed out that though rational deliberation is relative, there are many principles and values that have a great deal of stability. Like the "enabling beliefs" that we described earlier, such values as truth or goodwill are so fruitful in so many situations, and so flexible in their application to any conceivable new situation, that their chances of being repudiated by further inquiry are slim indeed. As Rescher says, "it is unlikely to the point of inconceivability that many of our historic social and personal values—'justice,' 'intelligence,' 'kindness,' to give just three examples—could ever, under any realistically foreseeable circumstances, lie open to valid negative criticism."[9]

WHAT ABOUT RELIGION AND WORLD-VIEWS?

A special problem for public education arises from the close relationship that world-views have to evaluation. Hare, in his work *The Language of Morals*, writes that "if pressed to justify a decision completely, we have to give a complete specification of the way of life of which it is a part." Though this complete specification is impossible to give in practice, he says, "the nearest attempts are those given by the great religions. . . ."[10]

A man's *religion* is his most general life-orientation, his steady estimate about what is real and valuable. In this sense, philosophical naturalism is as much a *religion* as Roman Catholicism. American law does not permit the public schools to support the establishment of any religion whatsoever. Therefore, it cannot be the trustee of any one world-view. Does this final barrier prevent the teaching of values in the schools? In answer to this question several distinctions need to be made.

First, the schools cannot represent any single world-view of either secular or official *religion*. There is no dispute about that, and even if it were not against the law, in a pluralistic democracy, there

[9] *Ibid.*, p. 140.
[10] Hare, *The Language of Morals*, p. 69.

would be no fair way to determine what the official view should be.

Though the schools cannot teach such world-views, they can teach *about* them. Public education may reasonably offer the student an appreciation of the various live options that human beings face in the modern world. Fortunately, a teacher need not espouse a world-view to understand and appreciate it. Teaching *about* world-views should include a comparison of differences and similarities. It is important for students who will be choosing one or another of such life-styles to have some appreciation for the decisions of others. In a democracy, this is the only way they will be able to work together for the common welfare without mutual suspicion and destructive conflict.

The effect of a national dialogue on such matters could also have a salutory effect on the organizations that represent these respective faiths. The mere fact of entering a dialogue of reason and imaginative sharing should incline rival faiths to develop a more adequate and publicly agreeable account of their own faith.

Finally, it may be noted that though values have their final synthesis in some world view, they are also often rooted in the common life with its common interests and problems so that agreement can often be reached at this level even when there are differences at a *higher* level. At present, for example, a substantial segment of Roman Catholic thought supports the basic premises of American democracy in agreement with the thought of both Protestants and Deweyan naturalists. Each group postulates its own metaphysical support for a common value, and that can only mean a wider consensus on an important public concern.

A FINAL WORD ABOUT
VALUES IN EDUCATION

Looking back over the argument of this chapter, it occurs to me that I have been so eager to make a case for the rationality of evaluation that despite many cavils I have not made enough of the complexities involved.

The terrain of evaluation is very complex, and philosophers have differed with one another about how it should be mapped. Some have emphasized moral values, others have argued that rules derive from such utilitarian principles as the greatest good of the greatest number. There is no single kind of argument to be used in a given case, but it is interesting that each of these philosophical points of view serve to illuminate some aspect of the good life. Stoicism, for instance, clarifies the kinds of principles that are our best resort when we are faced with circumstances that cannot be changed but must be endured with dignity. Pragmatism, on the other hand, illuminates procedures that are reasonable when problems can be resolved. Idealism often holds up values that are obscured by utilitarians, and utilitarians demonstrate the power of many common and pedestrian values to bring about agreement in moral disputes.

The merit of ordinary language analysis is that it can use the insights of these various schools as they are embodied in our linguistic usage. It keeps us from opting for implausible claims that outrage the wisdom embodied in our common speech and create a forum for the various trends of moral discussion.

The pluralistic nature of moral reflection strongly suggests the truth of Wittgenstein's remarks about a common family of meanings related in diverse ways rather than any single theory structured like geometry. At the present stage of philosophy, the rationale of moral decision making could very well commend itself to the educator.

The point is that there is a logic which defies simplification into a single set of rules or principles, but which can operate in practice to make choosing more rational. New observations and experiences will no doubt bring forth fresh principles or a vision of new values, allowing previous decisions to be amended and made more adequate. Adequacy, in this context, is tested in the satisfactoriness of human life itself, in human enrichment and enlargement. Since man's experience grows—and men grow with it—this enlargement is natural if not inevitable. It is not merely a random or whimsical affair. We can, without too much wisdom, see the difference between growth and deterioration in the choices that men make. Human maturity takes many forms, but most of them are recognizably superior to immaturity, though they may not all be equally meritorious. Inquiry into which forms of maturity are most fully human does not imply uncertainty about the value of maturity as such, and the dialogue among reasonable men about the various ideals of human existence should serve only to enlarge and elevate them.

A final thought: There is no reason, despite our contemporary perplexities, for giving in to skepticism or a moral nihilism which is usually a prelude to a despairing reliance on some dogmatic or narrow morality. If educators can bring themselves to deal with moral matters, calling upon other disciplines to support them in that task, there is at least a prospect that new generations of students disciplined in the rationale of evaluation might add a new dimension to the common life.

11

DEMOCRACY

To talk about analytic philosophy in education without dealing with the concept of *democracy*, insofar as it has a bearing on educational concepts, would be to ignore one of our deepest national concerns. America has big commitments to both democracy and education, and we have yet to see clearly how these commitments relate to one another. It would be a mistake, however, to suppose that philosophy in the analytic vein can function as advocate for programs or wise advisor on vexing problems. Its role must be more modest: that of a logical conscience continually seeking the clarification of meanings, exposing presuppositions, or showing the relationships between ideas.

WHAT IS "DEMOCRACY"?

An analytic answer to this question can neither begin nor end with abstract definitions of democracy. A good example of the analysis for which we are looking is to be found in Peters' *Ethics and Education*.[1] Peters argues that defining democracy simply as "rule of the people" is too vague and has little substantive meaning outside of some actual social system. A better approach, he suggests, is to examine the recent history of existing Anglo-American democracies and note their presuppositions. These systems came into being primarily as the result of a determination by the people of England and America not to be subject to arbitrary political authority. Peters says of the American Constitution, for example, that it is "one of the greatest monuments to rationality in the history of man," that it "represents an elaborate attempt to provide effective government within a system of checks and balances that were meant to safeguard the rights of individuals and of minorities against the possible tyranny of both the executive and the popular assembly."[2] In this, the Constitution is a descendent of the Magna Carta and other English institutions.

The presuppositions of the institutions that emerged out of these historical developments could be said to constitute the constellation of meanings that we call "democracy" in the Anglo-Saxon tradition. What are some of these presuppositions? (1) The first is that authority is conditional. (2) A second presupposition follows from this conditional acceptance of authority: a commitment to rational discussion in the process of making political decisions. Rational discussion in this context means something like what we have called the process of moral deliberation.

(3) It follows from the nature of such decision making that it cannot be assimilated to a mere polling of personal interests. If democracy were merely government by the wishes of a majority, some kind of computerized polling of interests could conceivably tabulate it better than the voting procedures presently used by democratic societies. However, a rule of majority wishes would be

[1] R. S. Peters, "Democracy and Education," in R. S. Peters (ed.), *Ethics and Education*, chapter 10.
[2] *Ibid.*, p. 199.

as arbitrary in its way as the will of an absolute sovereign. What is implied in Anglo-American democracy is something else: public *deliberation* on policy with a considered *judgment* as the conclusion. Such judgments, says Peters, cannot be spun out of the purely abstract concept of "the rule of the people."

(4) These procedures of *advise and consent* presuppose another condition, namely, some safeguards for the public expression of opinion, a freedom of the spoken and written word and voluntary assembly. If there were no such freedom, it would be vain to talk of consultation.

(5) Decision by consultation presupposes, moreover, some further procedures for public accountability. A democratic government must be kept constantly responsive to the process of consultation and judgment. That is to say, in principle, the government must be subject to change in an orderly manner. Democracy institutionalizes the process of governmental change so that the costly process of revolution may become unnecessary. This presupposes (6) that the people understand the nature of their government well enough so that there is a minimal consensus on procedural principles. Without agreement on fairness, respect for persons, the importance of considering everyone's interests, however bizarre, cooperation with other citizens, even those with which one disagrees, and the appeal to reason, public discussions would degenerate into propaganda and abuse. Perhaps, *understanding* is not an adequate term for this. One might almost say that we are talking about a popular *disposition* to participate in democratic processes in accordance with its rules.

These are then the presuppositions imminent in Anglo-American democratic institutions as they have developed concretely. Because this *democracy* emerged historically, it would appear likely that these procedures may not be imitated easily by peoples who have not had similar historical experiences. They are rational for people with a specific history, but they are not considered rightly as abstract ideals.

FURTHER PRESUPPOSITIONS OF DEMOCRACY

The foregoing discussion begins with the concrete historical institutions of Anglo-Saxon countries. It cannot be denied, however, that discussions of *democracy* in a wider sense have been going on since Plato. They raise some general philosophical questions that deserve some attention, particularly since they are part of current popular views on the subject.

The first concerns a doubt that human beings are capable of self-government. Plato's contempt for democracy as a "great beast" is still shared by many. Is the ideal of self-government unrealistic? We have seen that it is probably unrealistic without some propitious form of historical experience, but the wider question is one concerning human nature itself. Does democracy presuppose that men are more ideal than they actually are? Some of its defenders have made themselves vulnerable to this charge, but an accurate account of what self-government presupposes is somewhat more sober.

Self-government does not presuppose ideal men. It presupposes that no men are good enough to be trusted with unchecked power over other men. It denies there could be a group of men who could qualify in wisdom and goodness as Plato's philosopher kings. This is a presupposition of limits to general human wisdom and benevolence. It agrees with the axiom that power corrupts and absolute power corrupts absolutely.

Anglo-Saxon institutions, built upon the strategy of the separation of powers, and a continuous series of checks and balances, takes this weakness into account. It requires for every great power a countervailing power that will keep it from becoming tyrannical. This general proposition does not tell us what actual powers men ought to have, but only that they may not be trusted too far. It does not solve the practical problem that can emerge when the powers of a society are so counter balanced that necessary action cannot be taken, or taken in time. Reasonable principles do not absolve men from the work of forging viable institutions that exemplify those principles.

There is a counterproposition that is also part of the democratic creed, namely, that men are wise enough and good enough to make collective judgments about their welfare. There is no proof of this. It is simply a presupposition of this form of social life. If it is not true, however, the minimum degree of mutual trust, forebearance, and reasoned cooperation necessary for social existence will fail to materialize. Again, fortuitous social history may make this more likely at one time than at another. The minimum consensus may not be possible at certain junctures of history. These periods will inevitably run the risk of the unchecked misuse of power. It may be presumed that one of the tasks properly assigned to the schools of a democracy is the education of citizens with at least minimum qualifications for administering its major institutions.

Democracy, then, does not presuppose a utopian view of human nature. It presupposes that men are neither angels nor devils, but that they are capable at times of approximating both. Men can approximate moral rectitude and objective rationality in making judgments about the conflicts of human interests, but none of them is so free from the limitations of his own perspective that he can see everywhere equally. The possession of unchecked power reduces a person's need to consider the interests of others and therefore, to that degree, the likelihood of attaining impartiality in vision and judgment. Democracy is thus a theory of social organization that claims to approximate the nature of men as they actually are. It may strain their virtues, but it does not depend upon their perfectibility.

Democracy also presupposes some rationale to evaluation, some difference between desires and the desirable, between wishes and wisdom. Reliable values are not, as we contended in the last chapter, matters of mere subjective prejudice. They are capable of improvement if not perfection by rational determination. Philosophers who argue that democracy presupposes that there are no rational standards of moral or value deliberation are, I think, mistaken. This claim rests upon the argument that where there are no such standards, there is no reason to impose a system of values on anyone who does not agree with it. So far so good, but if there are no rational procedures for settling claims between conflicting groups, to what arbiter may men turn. If not to persuasive deliberation, it appears that arbitrary power becomes the only alternative. A society with no faith in deliberation could, at best, attain some kind of uneasy compromise depending upon the power of a given group to impose its will on the final determination. Such a society would become an arena of a power struggle unmitigated by any rational considerations except self-interest. Hans Reichenbach, who has argued for this view, might reply that, unfortunately, this is the way it is. This argument underestimates the case that can be made for reason in matters of morals and values. Reichenbach's view is a natural product of the positivism of the thirties and suffers from the limitations of that philosophical position.

This leads us into one of the difficulties inherent in any view of democracy that equates the voice of the people with the voice of God or the voice of truth. In cognitive matters, we know that this is not true. Legislatures or referendums cannot determine matters of fact, they can only register the prejudiced decision of majorities, but neither can majorities automatically determine warrantable judgments of value. Only rational deliberations can hope to reach such judgments. This means that whereas decisions will have to be made in some way responsive to majorities, the majorities must be restrained by the procedural agreements to which we have referred or democracy turns into the "Great Beast" of popular and ignorant opinion which Plato so rightly feared. Such a democracy may execute a Socrates or order the cremation of a racial minority. America is even now torn between a majority prejudice against her black citizens and her traditional institutions of democratic impartiality. Only if the majority of citizens is educated in the meaning implicit in her traditional institutions can this issue have any chance of a favorable outcome.

EDUCATION IN A DEMOCRACY

What would characterize a democratic educational system? Two things immediately suggest themselves: Education universally distributed and democratically organized. Neither of these was apparent to our immediate predecessors who fostered an education for the elite, governed by the elite. The elite in this case is the upper middle class who conceived of education in their own terms.

At the present time, these two democratic claims in education have come to the fore, not without dispute. The basic claim appears to be unanswerable. Any educational system that calls itself democratic may not exclude any minority from its benefits. Nor would we call it democratic if those involved in the system did not have some share in the decisions about how the system functions. Advise and consent must prevail in education as in politics.

Furthermore, almost as obvious is the fact that, as Peters says, "Without education an individual in a modern industrial society is unlikely to be able to proceed very far in developing the particular aspect of a worthwhile form of life to which he is suited; also an education system acts selectively in equipping citizens with skills and knowledge that are essential to the community's viability and development."[3] On the one hand, if the individual is to be given the opportunity to fulfill his own life, he must have access to the education he needs. On the other, society cannot function without skilled and knowledgeable citizens. This latter notion includes the fact that we noted a moment ago: Democracy is not viable as a social system without citizens who understand its institutions and values and who are disposed to abide by the principles implicit in them. One of the larger tasks of education in a democracy is thus the creation of the rational consensus on what Maritain calls the "democratic charter."[4] This does not mean, as Maritain points out, that everyone has to agree on a philosophy justifying these principles.

I have said "rational" consensus because education could not create this agreement by indoctrination or conditioning without ceasing to be an educational enterprise. It can reach for consensus only by bringing students to understand the principles and values involved and showing the inherent rationality of such a view of our common life. This consonance between the concepts of *teaching* and *educating*, as we have come to view them, and the *democratic charter* has been noted by Scheffler. He points out that although every culture has to renew itself through some kind of collective effort or die, it is not the case that it will necessarily do so through *teaching* in the standard sense. "To favor the widest diffusion of teaching as a mode and as a model of cultural renewal," Scheffler writes, "is, in, fact, a significant social option of a fundamental kind, involving the widest possible extension of reasoned criticism to the culture itself."[5]

[3] *Ibid.*, p. 208.

[4] Jacques Maritain, "Thomist Views on Education," in Nelson B. Henry (ed.), *Modern Philosophies and Education* (Chicago: University of Chicago Press, 1955), p. 72.

[5] Scheffler, "The Concept of Teaching," in Macmillan and Nelson (eds.), *Concepts of Teaching: Philosophical Essays*, pp. 18–19.

Democracy implies the possibility of large-scale change through public deliberation, a deliberation that cannot, in the nature of the case, be merely a head-count of personal interests. To quote Scheffler again: "To support the widest diffusion of teaching as a model of cultural renewal is, in effect, to support something that poses a threat to culture whose basic social norms are institutionally protected from criticism."[6] We have already noted that such a concept of education is not consistent with the kind of societies that emerged under Hitler and Stalin. This is a logical point. Cultural renewal through education, in our sense, presupposes something like an open democratic society, and, conversely, a democratic society presupposes the education of its citizens in the rationality of deliberation that is at the heart of *teaching*.

AUTHORITY

The problem of authority arises in education at three levels: (1) Where should authority over the whole system be vested? (2) What kind of authority can be justified in the local school? (3) What is the authority of the teacher?

The answer to the first question is clear: In the people. If an educational system is to be democratic, it must be responsive to their needs and desires. However, we meet the same problem that the American founding fathers faced with the Congress. If governmental policy was to represent considered judgment, not merely the momentary wish of a majority, then rational deliberation must somehow intervene between the act of consulting interests and determining policy. The same can be said of the people's control of education. Direct popular participation in educational decisions has not been altogether salutary in American communities. It has often taken the form of popular pressure against experimental or controversial programs. Often the result has been counter educational.

Two things are required: a forum where educational policies may be debated in a rational way and a corp of responsible edu-

[6] *Ibid.*, p. 19.

cators who will carry out educational policy in the light of that debate. Forming such institutions is not a philosophical affair. The following principle would seem to commend itself: Educational policy decisions should be placed neither too near the local school nor too far away. If it is too near, then the school is subject to the whim of every pressure group. If it is too far, then the popular interest will not be a significant component in the decisions. The present dogma that the local community should have control over the local school deserves critical reevaluation in the light of this principle. A school whose curriculum is merely the whim of local pressure groups is unlikely to be an educational institution. If there is no consultation with the local community, it will not be a democratic school system. What is needed is an arrangement that assures maximum consultation coupled with a maximum of rational deliberation before educational decisions are made.

AUTHORITY IN THE LOCAL SCHOOL

The second question, regarding the control of the local school itself, is also a proper concern for an educational system that calls itself democratic. The local school is not democratic if all the decisions about the conduct of teachers and students are made by a powerful principal. This is a surprisingly widespread practice. Where this is the case, the life of a school takes on the complexion of a prison run by an authoritarian warden. To be sure, a principal must be responsible for directing the institution, but he need not have the authority of a dictator. Students and teachers alike should be regularly consulted on the rules that control their miniature society. The consultation must be real. If debate is held only to discover that the principal has made the decision in advance, the result will be cynicism and rebellion on the part of both teachers and students.

A democratically run school would allow students considerable latitude in making the rules that control their behavior. Surely, teachers can be trusted to agree on the rules that should prevail concerning their own behavior while on the premises. If these freedoms are not observed, for what kind of democracy are the students being prepared? It is also a fact that the climate of such an authoritarian institution will very likely be restive and un-friendly, a climate not conducive to learning. The student will, furthermore, come to associate learning with an oppressive atmos-phere from which he longs to escape. Compulsory attendance will have already contributed its bit to this feeling, almost like a jail sentence, and must be consciously offset by the strategy of democratic participation and freedom. The teacher in turn will dislike playing the role of policeman and lose his zest for teaching. What must happen in teaching cannot be compelled in either the teacher or the learner. The more the atmosphere is one of con-genial cooperation and agreement, the better the chance of exciting teaching and of awakening the student's understanding.

Again, philosophy cannot propose the means to this happy possibility. All that analysis can do is to clarify the issues at stake. The solutions will always be relative to the kinds of teachers, administrators, and students in the school, coupled with the type of community in which it is set.

THE AUTHORITY OF THE TEACHER

There is no question but that the teacher must exercise authority of some kind. Leaving aside the question of his responsibility for order in his own classroom, let us examine his authority as a teaching agent. He should, of course, know more than his students about the subject he is teaching. His authority here is derived from his professional mastery of the knowledge relevant to that subject. One would expect from this a certain deference on the part of the student to the teacher, but the teacher's authority is a derived authority. It does not follow from the mere fact that the teacher is the teacher and the student is the student. It derives from the warranted findings in the subject being taught. This means that whenever the teacher decides some matter by virtue of his being an authority, the student has the right to ask why the decision was made in this way. A *teacher* must be able to give reasons. If he stifles questions, he conveys a false impression of his role and teaches a wrong-headed obedience on the part of the student. In today's environment, this response may very likely lead the student to reject the teacher's authority in toto, unless he has been trained to render unquestioning and obedient responses to commands. This could hardly be said to prepare a student for participation in a democracy, to say nothing of preparing him in the subject matter being taught.

I have urged that teaching lead the learner to understand and to respect his own powers of understanding. The needs of democracy underscore this even more. Therefore, a teacher must open the opportunity for students to question him and allow debate on why he says the things he does. Sometimes a teacher does not know the answer to a given question and thinks that if he admits as much, he will undermine his authority. The opposite is the case. Ignorance may be an invitation to group inquiry. It gives him the chance to say that he will reexamine what he has said. He need not apologize for not being omniscient. He may cite authorities to support what he has taught and yet admit that even this does not settle the question with finality. In *teaching*, there is no finality, though there is usually evidence that will satisfy a reasonable questioner.

Sometimes even after standard authorities are examined, the question is still not settled completely. This is an occasion to make the student aware that the answers are not complete, and that the student himself may add to the store of human learning if he is willing to prepare himself for the task. Education does not mean to find all the answers, but to discover how men come by answers that seem warrantable to them. Any given knowledge-claim is not infallible, it is a rationally assured claim that is infinitely better than the opinion of the ignorant. This temper of mind is itself good training for democracy for it creates an open mind at the same time that it teaches practical commitment. We cannot but commit ourselves to what we now believe to be warrantable knowledge, but we can still be open to further questions and the possibility upon some later occasion to change our commitments.

The hope of a *teacher* is to produce a student capable of critical thought. We need not concern ourselves further with this notion

as we have discussed the question of the meaning of *critical thinking* in several places. There is, however, a related question that
needs clarification, namely, the teaching of controversial subjects.

TEACHING CONTROVERSIAL SUBJECTS

At first sight the teaching of controversy would seem to upset
the necessary democratic consensus. If we look deeper, we discover that democratic consensus is not the same as agreement
on specific policies or programs. The consensus that supports a
democratic society is agreement on the democratic charter, the
charter that calls for freedom, deliberation, fairness, and so on.
That consensus is quite consistent with—and even productive of
—controversy. It is in controversy that the charter is tested and
made evident.

In a democratic society, the student may not be indoctrinated
into agreement. A student must understand the charter and agree
to disagree with others in the spirit of that charter. This opens a
whole range of disagreements on social programs, political parties,
and even religions, but in a fruitful way. It proceeds by rules
that give men some hope of living with their disagreements and
of resolving many of them.

Nor is this utopian. If the school sticks with the consensus
of the community at the level of politics and program, it will, in
the long run, nourish irrational outbreaks of strife in the life of
the community itself. Only if the citizens understand the spirit
of democratic disagreement—a disagreement that challenges every
way in which things might be done—can irrational strife be mini-
mized. The idea of democracy as aversion to irrational authority
carries with it the commitment to controversy. Almost everything
we have proclaimed as central to the educational enterprise supports the alliance of education and a society of intellectual open-
ness, continual reexamination, and rational deliberation. This is
in everyman's interest though he may not know it.

Democracy implies that no one man or faction sees everything
there is to see. Conservatives remind us of the richness of the
past, and liberals remind us of the danger of resting complacently

in the present. Dialogue among men of different perspectives is the very life of a democratic society. One obligation of the school is to make this clear to generations of future citizens. As soon as the conservative brands the liberal as a subversive radical, or the liberal abuses the conservative as a fascist reactionary, then the charter of democracy begins to give way to something entirely different.

EQUALITY AND QUALITY IN EDUCATION

Another problem facing the democratic educator is how to reconcile equality with quality in education. In his book *Excellence*, John Gardner asks, "Can we be equal and excellent too?"[7] He places in opposition two aphorisms acceptable to our culture: "All shall equal be." "Let the best man win." He cites Merle Curti on the Jacksonian era when equalitarianism reached absurd heights: "The democratic faith further held that no special group might mediate between the common man and truth, even though trained competence might make the difference between life and death. Thus in the West, even licensing of physicians was lax because not to be lax was apt to be thought undemocratic."[8] The problem lies at the heart of the democratic charter: on the one hand, equality and the commonweal, on the other hand, the person and his achievement. Actually, they are both needed. Without achievement on the part of individuals, without allowing the talented to rise and exercise their excellence, society itself would be deprived of the riches that come from those talents, but this is bought at the price of equality. Carried too far, a society is in danger of becoming elitist rather than democratic. A solution, if a dialectical tension can be called that, lies in moderating both the notion of equality and the notion of competitive achievement. "In its moderate forms," writes Gardener, "equalitarianism prohibits ruthlessness in the strong, protects the weak from wanton

[7] John Gardner, *Excellence* (New York: Harper & Row, 1961).
[8] *Ibid.*, pp. 13–14.

injury and defines certain areas of equality which must not be transgressed, but does not seek altogether to eliminate individual differences or their consequences."[9] The common man understands this in sports, but the hard task is to make it applicable to economic competition, politics, and in the other areas of social life.

The historical alternative to *achieved* status has always been *hereditary* status. The latter is in contradiction to democracy. Achieved status means a mobility upward for talent wherever it appears. In its raw form, it became, in nineteenth-century America, a crude social Darwinism. The point seems to be that a democracy dare not lose either achievement through performance or equality.

The problem of achieved status and the competition of ability lies chiefly in the fact that everyone in each generation does not start from the same place. In education, the culturally disadvantaged child generally cannot compete with his more advantaged colleagues regardless of his innate talents or capacities. Early in the game, he may become disheartened and drop out of the race altogether. Special classes for the disadvantaged may not seem like equality, but they are based manifestly on erasing an inequality that is present at the earliest stages of education. If society itself were not plagued by inequalities of income, housing, and so on, the school might not be faced with the problem. If education is to be democratic, it must try to make up, in its own sphere, what has been faulted elsewhere. If it succeeds in any measure, the educator will have helped in part, at least, to remedy the larger social inequity and contributed to the democratization of his society.

The same principle holds true for higher levels of education. An educational system that excludes students from college and university because of financial need cannot call itself democratic. The problem of admitting students who are culturally disadvantaged up through their high school years is a harder one to solve. Here again, a democratic system is commited by its nature

9 *Ibid.*, p. 15.

to attempt to mitigate this unjust consequence by special provisions until groups formerly excluded from the system can function within it more competitively.

In conclusion, we may observe that not only is a democratic view of society consistent with what we have come to understand by education, but that a democracy may be the only kind of society in which the full meaning of education can become manifest.

INDEX